Dreams

Dedicated to

Dream Forces, which bring
Peace and prosperity
On following days of our dreams

Dreams

As Foreshadows of the Future, Mirrored in Fantasies of the Present, and Fixations of the Past

Nandlal Vanvari

D.K. Printworld (P) Ltd.
New Delhi

Cataloging in Publication Data — DK
[Courtesy: D.K. Agencies (P) Ltd. <docinfo@dkagencies.com>]

Vanvari, Nandlal, 1940-
Dreams : as foreshadows of the future, mirrored in fantasies of the present, and fixations of the past / Nandlal Vanvari.
p. cm.
Includes bibliographical references (p.).
ISBN 13: 9788124604892 (Hb)
ISBN 10: 8124604894 (Hb)
ISBN 13: 9788124604908 (Pb)
ISBN 10: 8124604908 (Pb)

1. Dreams. 2. Dream interpretation. 3. Dreams — Dictionaries. I. Title.

DDC 154.63 22

ISBN 13: 978-81-246-0489-2 (HB) ISBN 10: 81-246-0489-4
ISBN 13: 978-81-246-0490-8 (PB) ISBN 10: 81-246-0490-8

First published in India in 2009

Published & printed by:
D.K. Printworld (P) Ltd.
Regd. Office: 'Sri Kunj', F-52, Bali Nagar
Ramesh Nagar Metro Station
New Delhi - 110 015
Phones: (011) 2545 3975; 2546 6019; *Fax*: (011) 2546 5926
E-mail: dkprintworld@vsnl.net
Website: www.dkprintworld.com

Preface

THROUGHOUT history, human beings have sought to understand the meaning of dreams. The ancient Assyrians, Babylonians, Egyptians, and Aryans believed dreams possessed oracular power. In the *Ramayana*, *Mahabharata*, Bible, and Koran, there are many many examples — the *Ramayana* has depicted a dream by a female demon about setting the whole Lanka on fire by a big monkey (Hanuman), and Sati Sulochana dreaming about the end of her husband Meghnada. *Mahabharata* tells that God told Vasudeva in dream to get up and take away Krishna who is born, immediately to save him from the wrath of his cruel maternal uncle Kansa, and another story about the dream of queen Gandhari manipulating the bodies of her hundred sons, who subsequently died in the Kurukshetra war. The Bible has given the example that Joseph's elucidation of Pharaoh's dream averted seven years of famine. Most of the Koran was handed over to Prophet Muhammad in a dream.

Dreams have been mystic experiences for evolved Souls. For some of them, dreams provided an alternative personality, such as prophetic speech, automatic writing, or the mediumistic trance.

Some shaggy scientific-minded cave dwellers began the study of the omens prophecies and warnings contained in dreams which have since been woven into the very fabric of life, until they have become a part of art, literature, and religion as well as science. Thereafter during the past century, scientists offered conflicting psychological and neuroscientific explanation: that dreams are a conglomerate of psychic formations in the psychic field of vision.

This book has been written to quench the curiosity, less of academic or historic nature and more of understanding, and application interests in practical life.

I present the text as a "tiny tot" in the field of dreams, who has picked up the pebbles from the playground of peers and principals of schools of dreams, and also from the seashore of Cosmic-Consciousness.

Contents

Introduction

DREAMS have fascinated mankind for ages and in spite of advances in psychological studies, the truth behind the mess of jumbled images which flood the mind when we sleep has not been adequately brought to light.

The ancient Egyptians believed dreams possessed oracular power. Other cultures have interpreted dreams as inspirational, curative, or alternative reality. Yet other views are:

— Although dreams might at times have psychological contents, they were inherently meaningless.

— Dreams are the means by which brain rids itself of unneccessary information.

— Every important occurrence in our lives is foreshadowed in our dreams.

— Dreams are a series of images and/or thoughts passing through the mind in sleep.

Everybody dreams; even a child of 8 months dreams; a low intelligence person dreams as much as a person with high intelligence; and a person who is blind since birth also dreams.

An unenlightened person is dreaming constantly, even when he is awake. S/he does not know this because her/his sensory functions are extroverted. The moment you cut-off your awareness from the sensory functions of sight, smell, sound, taste and touch, and relax, you begin to witness the dreams. The mind of a human being is dreaming all the time, consciously as well as unconsciously. The dreams during siesta and night-sleep are only a small part of this totality — a subject of the present text.

In this usual state of dreaming, the content and expression of dreams are related to the spontaneous build-up and release of psychic tension from the subconscious as well as the awakening and expression of the unconscious.

A normal person may not rely on dreams fully, whereas a person with developed consciousness, accepts dreams as "conscious facts," and carries them from present to future by his/her "free will."

Dreams are displays of your subconscious and unconscious, which know everything of the past, the present and the future, and also constitute an interrelation between the future, the now, and the past of human experience.

Dreams provide understanding of the present, and the basis for the future — the world yet unformed! Dreams have adumbrated the way we can avoid the evils of the present and the further evils yet to come in the future.

Dreams as Foreshadows of the Future

In dreams our objective senses have withdrawn into rest or oblivion. Then we are living alone in the future or ahead of objective life and consequently, we live our future first. Thus the dreams are forecasts — foreshadows of the future.

Dreams are an important window through which one can see his/her development and evolution, and take guidance from time to time. As you evolve, the cosmic energy within you changes in four stages: ignorance, sex, love and spriritual experience. This development is reflected in your dreams through the changing forms of anima, a female figure, if you are male; or of animus, a male figure, if you are a female. The exemplary characters are given in Table I[1] (modified by the author).

1. W. James, *The Varieties of Religious Experiences*, New York: New American Library of World Literature, 1958.

Table I : Phase of Evolution

S.No.	Cosmic Energy	Anima	Animus
1.	Primitive (Ignorance)	Eve	Tarzan
2.	Romantic (Sex)	Cleopatra	James Bond
3.	Loving (Love)	Mother Teresa	Mahatma Gandhi
4.	Spiritual (Soul)	Mona Lisa	Shirdi Sai Baba

Dreams reflect the facts of mental evolution and can foretell our coming triumps or disaster — display *deja vu,* premonitions, precognitions or prophetic visions.

The future has written down its facts and warnings, and this is solely due to nervous excitability of the subject whose brain has been the battlefield of many a strong presentiment, of many a dream oftrepeated, though totally forgotten on the morrow. These peculiar forebodings, which come to us without our full consciousness being awakened, exert at the time a sufficiently powerful influence upon the brain to cause it to send it down, as an important message, to its display device in the form of dreams; and there it is inscribed in letters and images and symbols mysterious, not as the edict of a dark, revengeful fatality, but as precious warnings to be heeded and acted upon by our wisdom and will-power.

Dreams as Fantasies of the Present

Our daily actions, transactions and reactions find their reflections as dreams in the mirrors of our minds, and dream fantasies are like mirrors that reflect our original nature with such a transparency that we are inherently safeguarded from being imprisoned in any form of conceptually fabricated understanding, however subtle, or convincing, or seductive.

Thus, dreams embody the fantasies and wishes that lie unknown and hidden within us, and represent a critical mean path (CPM) to our deeper feelings.

During sleep, our "will" is suspended, so the dreaming mind is more a prey to excitability and fantasy. Then, dreams can highlight our wishes and fears; can help to expose problems which we cannot face consciously. Essentially, dreams put us in touch with our own imaginations, which in turn create most of our dreams. Imagination, most of the time wild, allows us to inject dynamism into our lives. Imagination only gives us the courage to move forward, to grow. It is a fount of desire which is a fount of intent and achievement. Our dreams keep us moving, and offer us fantastical visions that complement our existence. Many humans seem to possess a "shadow" — a fantasy personality that is only revealed in dreams or under hypnosis or drug abuse. And, this "fantasy personality" is not the recollection of a previous life as such but a dream imagination of being a celebrity — in dreams people do imagine themselves to be famous persons.

The dreams are not only reflections of the fantasies of mind but also of all events of days and months which could be easily classified as of the "present."

Our fantasies do incorporate our ambitions. A careful analysis of the fantasies will enable you to make a distinction between consciously constructed dreams (ambitions) and sleep dreams.

It is good to be a dreamer but bad to go by wild dreams; it is better to be realistic — to come down to the realities of this world — rather than live in the fanciful fantasies of the "other world," that commands common sense too.

We know, woven into our present are images of our past that flash time and again during daydreaming or in dreams during night-sleep.

Dreams as Fixations of the Past

Each dream is a medley of some qualities that are heritages of the animal past and some which are seeds of a diviner future.

However, most of the dreams are uniformly the resuscitation or re-embodiment of thoughts which have formerly in some shape or other occupied the mind. They are old ideas revived either in an entire state or heterogeneously mingled together.

The past fixations, which are stored as conscious memories, reappear literaly. Such dreams are those that show the dreamer a dynamic replay of the previous events, s/he had faced. These dreams fetch her/him another opportunity to analyse the dream from a different outlook. These dreams may carry a hidden solution to our present problem.

Our dreams include snippets from childhood activity, old conversations, and places and objects that have nothing to do with our present-day circumstances.

Fearful encounters in our present and past lives are etched out forever, and they find a place in our dreams invariably and sometimes repeatedly.

Acording to Tantra, each and every perception, experience and association is recorded. If you have a quarrel or bitter exchange, that is very strong registration. However, if you happen to pass someone on the path, look at him and walk on, this is also registered. Many things come within your range of association, and they are all automatically registered. They are not analysed, but simply filed away in some layer of the mind. All those insignificant and unimpressive *karmas* (actions), which have been registered automatically in our consciousness, form the total unconscious — which comes up in dreams.

> The dreaming mind recalls past impressions.
> It sees again what has been seen; it hears
> Again what has been heard, enjoys again
> What has been enjoyed in many places.
> Seen and unseen, heard and unheard, enjoyed
> And unenjoyed, the real and the unreal,
> The mind sees all; the mind perceives all.
> — Sage Pippalada (The *Prashna Upanishad*)

Dream Phenomenon

Dreaming whether of the past, the present, or the future, is a mysterious phenomenon.

Life as granted to us has an in-built provision for a mental mutation which makes dreams possible. Had there not been the phenomenon of a dream how could we have conceptualized such a possibility? All the imaginings and fancies and fantasies of a waking mind would have rested in the direct identity of oneself, and would have never approached the magic and mystery of the metamorphosis of the waker into the dreamer.

Just as we live out our emotions, fantasies, strategies, and episodes in dreams, and till such time as a dream lasts it is reality, and we allow the dream to take its course, trying to come out of it only if it turns into a nightmare, so is the case with our lives. Just as, only after we awake and gauge our past, present and future life, we do find the dream was not our true life, but was a miniscule experience of our mind (real all the same) apart from our true life and with only a momentary repercussion on it, so also, at a very highly developed stage, when we can perceive the past, the present and future lives, we do realize that this life is also like a dream, a tiny episode in a long cycle of lives, leaving only a momentary repercussion on it. Till then, this life is reality, to be endured, just as the dream was a reality and had to be gone through.

Nevertheless, time-space transcendence of dreams, cultural and social barrier over-bridgings, is a common phenomenon during the night-sleep.

Also, we take a journey into the unmanifested every night, when we enter the phase of deep dreamless sleep. We merge with the Source. We drew from it the vital energy that sustains us for a while when we return to the manifested — the world of separate form. Thus energy is much more vital than food: "Man does not live by bread alone." Try to remain conscious during the dreamless sleep to draw more and more vital energy and get plugged into the Source — to walk on to the spiritual path. One can remain conscious during the dreaming sleep, whereas to remain conscious during the deep sleep is a difficult task, and only very highly evolved souls are able to do so.

Dr Bruce Goldberg,[2] clinical hypnotist from U.S.A., has claimed that events experienced in the third dimension should be conceived as a "past condition" because the conventional spatial universe is a projection or correlative of what is actually being built at an altogether higher level of existence. Consequently, turning into the higher levels, as dreaming can enable us to do, awakens us to the more profound, underlying reality of what is actually being built and can alert us to what may soon be projected into the physical realm in the future.

2. Bruce Goldberg, *Soul Healing*, New Delhi: Pustak Mahal, 1999.

1

Historic Dreams

ONLY history, that wayward and fickle daughter of time, tells about the dreams that have been cryptographed in books; some of which are given below:

- Olympias, the mother of Alexander the Great, dreamed her son would be a great leader whose empire would rise and fall.
- A German chemist Friedrich August von Kekule (1829-96) dreamed in one of the afternoons of 1865: the atoms gambolling before his eyes, and one of the snakes eating its own tail, thus forming a large ring. The dream inspired him to run tests which led to the discovery that the atoms in the benzene (C_6H_6) molecule were, in fact, arranged in a large ring of six interconnected carbon atoms — rather than the straight line arrangement previously visualized. To make the structure compatible with carbon's valency of four, he postulated alternate single and double bonds in the hexagonal ring.
- Russian chemist Dimitri Ivanovich Mendeleyev (1834–1907) solved the problem of constructing the periodic table, a problem with which he had been preoccupied for some time. As he was dozing while listening to chamber music, he realized in the dream that the basic elements were related to each other like melodies.
- Abraham Lincoln, President of America (1861-65), had seen himself been shot in some big public place four years before

his death. Lincoln had told about the dream to a close pal, Ward Hill Lamon, who had penned down the same in his diary.

It turned out to be the Ford's theatre where John Wilkes Booth shot him dead in the presence of the full house.

- Journalist W.T. Stead was aboard the Titanic, which sank in April 1912 off Newfoundland, with loss of 1513 lives. It was 20 years since he had penned a fictional story (based on premonition or dreams?) about an ocean liner (Titanic) which was crippled and sank after being breached by an iceberg. The story depicted himself as a shipwreck victim stranded in icy waters, shouting for help before slipping beneath waves — unwittingly Stead had graphically described his own fate.
- Carl Gustav Jung (1875–1961), a psychiatrist by profession but a psychic by nature, saw a dream three days before his death — a storm tore across Lake Geneva and lightning struck his favourite tree. His death occurred in Zurich on 6 June 1961, exactly as dreamt.
- Albert Einstein (1879–1955) had a dream, he was sleighing down a mountainside at the speed of "Light." He noticed that the stars refracted light into a spectrum of colours. Einstein maintained that thinking deeply about this dream brought him to the theory of relativity.
- During the first World War Adolf Hitler had a dream when he was sleeping in a bunker. He saw debris and earth falling upon him, crushing and suffocating him. Soon he awoke and ran outside the bunker in that chilly night. As he stood at a distance, a shell hit the bunker killing all the occupants. To Hitler, this was a divine providence.
- Mohammed Qaddafi survived the bombing of his tent in April 1986 by U.S. Forces, because he left the place a few minutes earlier, alarmed by warning in his sleep — a dream thought!
- One of the more recent examples is that of physiologist Otto

Loewi who dreamed one night (in 1920) of an experiment which might prove his theory concerning the transmission of nerve impulses. He set up the experiment in his laboratory exactly as he had dreamed it, and it worked, subsequently leading to Loewi's receiving the Nobel Prize in 1936.

- One of Australia's eminent film directors, George Miller, and his three brothers received many creative ideas during their daydreaming sessions. And, it is because of the film ideas so received that George Miller has reached the pinnacle in film direction.

- Dreams of the Aberfan, Wales, U.K. tragedy were foreseen by some sixty persons, some of whom were later victims of the disaster. It happened on 21 October 1966, that a huge stockpile of coal refuse collapsed and buried a school under it in a small mining village of Aberfan, killing more than 140 people including 128 school children.

  Sometimes a number of people will even have forebodings of the same event. Many of them have no direct connection with the tragedy they foresee; but some like Eryl Mai Jones became its victims.

  On 20 October 1966, this 9-year-old Welsh girl told her mother she had dreamt that when she had gone to school, it was not there."Something black had come down all over it," she said. Next day her mother witnessed the death drama in which the dreamer child was also killed.

- The Prime Minister of England, Spencer Percival, was shot dead in the House of Commons on 11 May 1812. An elderly gentleman living at Cornwall dreamt the entire incident thrice in succession and scene by scene, some eight or nine days before the assassination — a record that is well authenticated. That is not all. A few days before his death the prime minister himself had strong forebodings about the coming events, and promptly handed his will to his wife.

2

Views on Dreams

MANY celebrities and savants have given their views about dreams, which are useful to know in order to firm up our opinion of dreams. Some of these are:

- Dream is past, expectations of the future and cognitive perception of the present. — Aristotle
- Some say that gleams of remoter world visit the Soul in sleep. — Dante
- All dreams of the Soul end in a beautiful man's or woman's body. — W.B. Yeats
- Dream is spacious sky where lovers encounter comfort and condolence. — Anand Vanvari
- It is in our idleness in our dreams that the submerged truth sometimes comes to the top. — Virginia Woolfe
- The timeless in you is aware of life's timelessness, and knows that yesterday is but today's memory and tomorrow is today's dream. Trust the dreams, for in them is hidden the gate of eternity. — Kahlil Gibran
- The fusion of spiritual and physical memories is called a "dream." — Swami Atmananda
- Man also produces symbols, unconsciously and spontaneously in the form of dreams. — C.G. Jung
- A dream is a wish your heart makes. — Unknown

- Dream is an insubstantial pageant, and the dream-world is less rational. — Sir Arthur Stanley Eddington
- A dream is a film. A dream that is vulgar, stupid, dull and shapeless; it is perhaps a nightmare. Still, at least a dream is never an illusion. — Orson Welles
- I can never decide whether my dreams are the result of my thoughts or my thoughts are the result of my dreams. — D. H. Lawrence
- Dreams translate into thoughts, and thoughts translate into action. — A.P.J. Abdul Kalam
- I am captivated more by dreams of the future than by the history of the past. — Thomas Jefferson
- Those who dream by day are cognizant of many things which escape those who dream only by night. — Edgar Allan Poe
- Dreams are the touchstones of our character. — Henry David Thoreau
- All that is sometimes to make you content with your lot is a bad dream. — Michel Simon
- The skilful interpreter of dreams is he who has the faculty of observing resemblances. — Aristotle
- Those dreams that on the silent night intrude,
And with false flitting shades our mind delude,
Jove never sends us downward from the skies;
Nor can they from infernal mansions rise;
But all are mere productions of the brain,
And fools consult interpreters in vain. — Swift
- A dream is the royal road to the unconscious. — Dr A.A. Brill
- Dreams make an upward traffic between the conscious and the unconscious. — Arthur Koestler
- A dream is a purely mental idea. — Bishop Berkeley

- In dream-vision unconscious thought weds facts.
  — James Clerk Maxwell
- Who could be more original than a lunatic, and what is more imaginative than a dream. — Sir Cyril Burt
- Dreams are but the ideas of all poetic arts.
  — Herder, German Philosopher
- Dreams are involuntary experiences leading to the composition of poetry. — Jean Paul Richter
- The dreamer and his dream are the same . . . the powers personified in a dream are those that move the world.
  — Joseph Campbell
- Dreams open up unconscious resources, giving birth to the genius, jesters, artists, scientists, and spiritualists.
  — Nandlal Vanvari
- Dream and reality are virtually indistinguishable.
  — Peter Reich
- Dreamers of today are achievers of tomorrow. And forever they are dreamers who make their dreams come true.
  — Orison Swett Marden
- Whatever the inward darkness may have been to which the shamans descended in their trances, the same must lie within ourselves, nightly visited in our sleep (dreams).
  — Joseph Campbell
- He who goes to bed hungry, dreams of cakes.
  — Maltese Proverb
- We are such stuff as dreams are made on.
  — Shakespeare (The Tempest IV:1)
- Great dreamers' dreams are never fulfilled, they are always transcended. — Alfred Lord Whitehead
- The dream sleep is a kind of meditation. — N. Vanvari

- Dreams create known and unknown,
  Unidentified flying objects (UFOs),
  Psychosomatic diseases and matters,
  Enlightened Souls and even God. — N. Vanvari

- A dream within your dream
  portends a definite improvement
  in your present circumstances. — Tom Corbet

- A dream is "seeing" with closed eyes,
  which may be auspicious or inauspicious.
  — Baidyanath Saraswati

- A dream is nothing but passing out of
  the realm of thought, reason and philosophy
  into the shadow-and-fantasy land of . . .
  mysticism, where the heavy scent of
  beautiful poison flower drugs the
  intellect and obliterates thought
  in a blissful languorous repose. — Nandlal Vanvari

- Dreams are images perceived, when brain discharges its pent-up electric potentials. — Nitin Trasi

- The only remedy to heal a wound caused in a dream is to awaken. — Jñāneśvar

- Dreams are manifestations of mind,
  by mind, for mind. The mind
  has a personality in the dreams. — Nandlal Vanvari

- A dream is a fertile ground
  for flowering of extra-sensory perceptions. — N. Vanvari

- When dreams acquire the wings
  of idealism and are propelled
  by idea about history-transforming
  mission, they begin to soar far and high. — L.K. Advani

- Dreams may have sharp
  boundaries or fading frontiers. — N. Vanvari

3

Understanding Dreams

A CREATIVE life is rooted in an insight and the understanding of available information, environs, and the laws of nature. Let us have the understanding of dreams.

Dreams are mysterious processes to experience and to see through space and time. They are just like mini-micro TV serials, in which we act, with an audience of one (ourself): "They are fantastic and romantic, evolving or dissolving, comic and tragic; with fun or fears, smile of seers, and/or touch of tears." However, the boundaries of the self are fluid or blurred in a dream. One may watch an execution, and the next moment become the person to be executed. The actors on the stage are interchangeable; their cards of identity are often reshuffled. In dreams, the coherence of image frames is so much loosened that the change is not experienced as such, and side-stepping becomes almost the normal way of the dream's progress. For example, a cloud may resemble a camel, weasel or whale; to the dreamer the cloud actually becomes a camel, a weasel or the whale — without his/her turning even a hair — by mental quantum-jumps, as it were.

The percentage of dreams relating to our five senses, according to Professor W.S. Monroe's analysis, is as follows:

Sight impressions — in 63 per cent.

Hearing impressions — in 26 per cent.

Smell impressions — in 05 per cent.

Touch impressions — in 05 per cent.

Taste impressions — in less than 01 per cent.

of the dreams on an average level. During dreams neuro-motors are off, i.e. no walking, talking, crying, weeping, lifting, writing, reading, etc. However, sleep-walking, shouting, sweating, shock-shutting-of-dream-screen are recurring features.

Further a U.S. philosopher has observed that our dreams are monochrome. In surveys from 1950s — the age of black and white — most said that their dreams were never or rarely in golden colour, found Eric Schwitzgebel of University of California. U.S.A. Before and since, most have reported colourful dreams. Dreams are but chimerical fancy.

Colour of Dreams

Colour of a dream is linked with many things, viz. its atmosphere, mood, or feeling and food consumed at night. A grey display scene denotes a dull illusion, while a bright sunshine offers a message of hope, although, some displays may be assortments of different colours. Significance, according to major colour contents of a dream, is as follows:

- Violet — Indicates nostalgia and memories, also emotions.
- Indigo — Symbolizes "heart ruling head" syndrome.
- Blue — Symbolizes devotion, religious feelings and high aspirations of the Soul. Deep blue signifies intuition.
- Green — Signifies fertility, abundance, sympathy and adaptability, and can also signify cycles of decay and regeneration. Muddy green stands for jealousy.
- Yellow — It is associated with generosity financial prosperity, intuition and intellect, and the warmth of the sun. A muddy yellow indicates cowardice and "flight" syndrome.
- Orange— Symbolizes the dawning of spirituality, hope and new beginnings. It presages health, occult powers,

and psychic messages.

- Red — Signifies passion, sentiments, fire and blood; it is vital, passionate colour, also associated with sexual arousal, sensuality and anger.

Besides the above rainbow colours, dreams are also displayed in a variety of other colourations, such as:

- Purple — It is associated with power, regality, and richness.
- Pink — It is colour of flesh; it symbolizes love, emotions, vulnerability and sensuality.
- White — Symbolizes magic, purity, celestial bodies (the stars and the moon), caring and recovery.
- Grey — It is associated with ashes and can signify depression, inertia and indifference, it can also be associated with egotism.
- Black — It is associated with earth, darkness and the occult. It signifies death and depression.
- Brown — Symbolizes sensation and sometimes disintegration.
- Golden — Signifies conscious mind and truth.
- Silver — Presages wisdom, peace and light.

In general, bright and clear colours are indicative of positive aspects or trends in our lives while muddy or drab colours have negative orientation.

Even though dreams may actually occur in colour, they often fade to black and white, when you recall them.

Sleep and Dreams

Sleep on set insomnia is basically the inability to fall asleep. A typical run-in with insomnia is that you have been lying in your sleeping position for the past hour or so. Your body is tense, a solid knot of muscle. Your mind is spinning at high speed with random, mostly self-defeating thoughts — a myriad of past, present, and future problems. In the midst of all this turmoil and unrest, your eyelids keep flipping open. The pillow seems too high, too low, too hard, too soft. At some time during the night the sheets turn to sandpaper. Someone has sucked all the air out of the room. You start noticing noises you never heard before.

Medical experts assert that if insomnia is not in the disease state, at night you will doze off to sleep within 20 to 30 minutes.

All living beings sleep — an opossum sleeps for 20 hours, pythons sleep for 18 hours, cats for 12 hours, horses for three hours, and giraffe sleeps for two hours only. Whereas human infants sleep for 16 hours, adults for about 8 hours, and old for only 3 to 5 hours.

Every night when we sleep we die. We lose awareness of the world and ourselves only to be reborn to the dawn of next day. In yogic terminology the *jiva*, the individual consciousness, sinks through the physical, pranic and mental bodies to rest in the causal body — remains there in altered state of consciousness in semi-unconscious or unconscious form. Occasionally, it comes up into the psychic body to dream.

Dreams of old and adults are vivid, virile, vermicular, verdant, venturous and/or venerable, whereas, the dreams of young children are often so short, yet clear, coherent, and easy to understand that very little in the way of interpretaion is needed.

The sleep starts with NREM (no rapid eye movement) phase followed by REM (rapid eye movement) phase. If the sleeper is snoring during NREM sleep, s/he stops snoring once the REM sleep phase begins. The REM phase is followed by NREM phase. Thus, NREM-REM cycles are taking place during the night-sleep.

The first REM sleep phase usually lasts about ten minutes. The following REM phases progressively grow longer. The final REM period immediately before we wake up, lasts for between 20 and 40 minutes. It is during REM phases that one dreams, and each REM phase may have at least one dream.

The sleep cycle — alternating NREM and REM sleep — appears to be present in all placental and marsupial mammals. Mammals exhibit the various REM-associated characteristics observed in humans, including EEG (electro-encephalo graphic) readings similar to those of the awaken state. Animals also dream. By destroying neurons in the brain stem that inhibit movement during sleep, researchers found that sleeping cats rose up and attacked or were startled by invisible objects — ostensibly images from dreams. Prey-animals dream less; their predators dream more, like lions enjoy dreaming of eatables.

Sleep during the day (nap) may be either due to fatigue, regular practice or out of contemplation for daydreaming. The daydreaming helps in solving difficult problems and boosting creativity. Dreaming (during night) is distinguished from daydreaming (and reverie) in that the dreamer is aware of fantasies which he creates, but unware of the fact that he is creating them. He is the spectator passively watching the sequence of images on one level, which he actively produces on another; he acts as the cinema operator who works the projection machine, and the audience at the same time. But while the spectacle on the screen is visible, the operator is not. He operates in complete darkness, and there is good reason for it: the production is frequently childish, obscene, confusing, an affront to logic and common sense.

The content of "daydreams" and of "siesta-dreams" is so apparently meaningful and the content of "night-dreams" is so typically bizarre. Day dreams are, in fact, transparent wish-fulfilments in which the subject, himself/herself, is either the hero/heroine or obviously identified with the central character — the fantasies.

As we fall asleep our breathing slows down; the pulse rate and body temperature both drop and the muscles relax. During REM phase, blood pressure rises, heart beat increases, and forehead temperature rises. In the NREM sleep phases, one gets the most rest, whereas REM sleep is information processing period — memories and events of the day are juxtaposed with the things that happened in the past to form a strategy for survival, invariably.

According to tantrics, dreams, sleep, higher psychic and causal functions are modulated by our seven *chakras*. For an ordinary dreamer, the *prana* (breath — bio-plasmic energy) remains in the fourth *chakra* (heart *chakra*) during dreaming and in the fifth *chakra* (throat *chakra*) during the deep sleep.

However, in those persons who are highly evolved, the *pranas* rest in the 6th *chakra* (third eye *chakra*) during the experience of dream and vision, and in the 7th *chakra* (crown *chakra*) during deep sleep.

While dreaming we constantly bisociate in passive way — by drift as it were; but we are, of course, unware of it beacuse the coherence of logical matrices is weakened, and the codes which govern them are dormant. Hence, while dreaming we do not realize their incompatibility; there is no simultaneous juxtaposition of matrices, no awareness of conflict and incongruity; that comes only on awakening.

Most dreaming occurs during REM sleep phases, when our awareness can transcend space and time. During REM sleep, our large muscles are completely paralyzed. We cannot walk or talk. Conversely, most of our brain cells are vigorously active. Among them are cells in our motor centres, a phenomenon, that may explain sensations of movements such as the ability to fly in dreams. Nerve cells that govern motivation and logic, however, turn off during REM; consequently most dreams are involuntary and amnesic. The dream in last REM sleep phase is most often recalled.

Normally during our eight hours sleep there will be four NREM-REM cycles, but in certain cases there may be up to seven cycles per night. With 4 to 7 NREM-REM cycles, the number of dreams should be 4 to 7. Scientifically, the dream number has been established to be three to nine per night. Further, as each and every minute in the REM cycle is equal to three to four clock minutes, thus the dreaming process is three to four times faster than the speed of light (three to four times faster than your response time on a phone across the globe). That is why in no time a dream scene, shifts between different worlds — actually it shifts with the speed of "thought," which may be many many times the speed of "light."

The onset of sleep is marked by short visions and images called "hypnogogic" dreams. Then follows "hypnopompic" state of dreaming. During hypnogogic (waking and sleeping) and hypnopompic (sleeping and waking) states, dreaming sensation is available:

> What we wish to recognize is that apparently a terrible species of wild and lawless appetites resides in everyone of us, even when in some cases we have the appearance of being perfectly self-restrained. And this fact, it seems, becomes evident in sleep. — Plato

Plato, an eminent Greek philosopher, propounded a theory that dream is like a cake of wax; that it resides in the dark interior of one's mind (known as "unconscious"). The shape, size, density and malleability of this waxen cake would decide the strength and clarity of the impression that would be etched on it.

If a person sleeps really soundly or very deeply, therefore, s/he probably will not dream. This does not mean necessarily that if you don't recollect dreaming you have slept soundly, for more often than not we do not remember our dreams. The more lightly you sleep, however, the more likely you will dream or tend to remember what you have dreamed.

For most people, the contents of the dreams and deep sleep states are glimpsed only in a haphazard way by the conscious mind through occasional recall of a dream, trance, or vision. Even these are often so highly symbolic and archetypal that they are not understood by the conscious mind and therefore remain unintegrated.

"We are somewhat more than overselves in sleep, and the slumber of the body seems to be but the waking of the Soul," Sir Thomas Browne wrote thirty-four decades ago. Yet it is difficult and frustrating to write consciously on the unconscious, rationally on the irrational. It is rather like praising the beauties and expounding the grammar of the Sanskrit language — but a Sanskrit which you speak only in your sleep and the command of which you lose when awake. Only fragments of it emerge to the surface — disjointed memories and the testimonies of creative minds. When these fragments are pieced together, as best as we can, they do not form a coherent picture — but they do provide evidence that such a picture exists.

Soul and Dreams

A human is a composite of body, mind and soul. The "soul" is a subtle body having the same shape and size of the physical body to which the soul belongs. It is dynamic with supernatural powers. It is desirable, however, to further define the soul. The subtle body having the same shape and size dies within 12 hours of the death of the physical body, whereas the dynamic essence never dies — it is the "Soul," which moves on.

The mind lies between the soul and the physical body, so that a person experiences space-time continuum in the flexible, plastic form we know best in dreams, and also in some extrasensory perceptive experiences.

Tertutlin (CE 160–240), a Christian bishop held the view that like the body the soul took nourishment during sleep, but of a different kind, consisting of dreams. Dreams were natural and in them revelations might be made of medical treatment, hidden treasure, stolen goods, of future honours; demons might cause impure, frivolous or turbulent dreams; and vision containing sacred prophecy might proceed from holy angels.

The Indians of Guiana believe that a person sleeps or wakes according to whether his/her soul is abroad or in the body. The soul is away to witness a dream scene. According to them, waking up is the sign of the soul's return. Any interference with the returning of the soul to the body may prove fatal. It is an offence for a member of the Miningkabauen tribe of Sumatra to stain the face of any sleeper, because it would confuse the returning soul. The Patani Malays say that the confuse soul will not return to a painted sleeper until the paint is washed off.

The Koreans firmly believe that the scenery of dreams is derived from the experiences of their soul. They further believe that the soul cannot frequent a place unless the soul has visited the place earlier. But, the Maoris think that soul can visit any place any time. So is the view of all other races that soul can travel beyond time, space and speed limitations.

According to the Choctaw Indian's belief each person has two spirits (souls), one the internal and the second external (called shadow) — they call them "Shilup" and "Shilombish" respectively. They claim that only "Shilup" survives after death. It is "Shilombish" which travels to bring the dreams. The Fijians believe that the shadow which they call the "Dark Spirit" leaves the body after death to the unknown world and the "Light Spirit" continues to haunt the place where the death has taken place.

So far as the place of exit and entry for the soul, on its nocturnal excursions from the body during dreaming (or during near-death-experience, out-of-body experience, astral travel, or Shamanic flights) is concerned there are different views in different countries. Old Germans believed that it was the mouth, the soul taking the form of a little bird or white mouse went out or returned only when the mouth was open. In Transylvania everyone was warned never to sleep with the open mouth, for the soul should slip out like a mouse and abandon the sleeper, who would die. Other cultures believed that the soul is tied to the physical body's navel or the place between the eyebrows with a silver cord of an infinite length.

The materialists — the Charvakas in India and the Epicureans in Greece — denied the soul. They said "There is no soul. The soul is just imagination. The soul is an illusion." And the Spiritualists — Shankaracharya in India and Berkeley in Europe — say matter is illusory, *maya*. The body does not exist really, it is only your imagination. It is a dream, made of the same stuff as dreams are made of; you are a soul. But both are agreeing on one point: that they cannot accept reality as it is, they have to choose between dreams and reality.

Nevertheless, dreams are the whispers of the soul and relay crucial information that prompts us on the path to better living and life.

Mind and Dreams

A dream, no matter what distortions, anomalies, exaggerations or absurdities it accommodates, is entirely a product of the dreamer's mind. The propensities of his mind, evident or subliminal, shaped by his memories and preferences, fashion the dream without any contribution or contamination from external factors.

Living matter is a part of nature, having the vital property of memory, perception, knowledge and consciousness. Human life is considered to be evolved. Since it possesses the capacity to embody a separate sense called "mind" along with other senses (touch, taste, smell, sound and sight), through this composite medium of cognition one can perceive the images of nature.

Dr Yatish Agarwal,[1] a noted physician from India, says:

> The human mind is simply awesome. With cranium for its abode, a 1350 grammes mushroom of grey and white tissue of gelatine-like consistency and 100 billion nerve cells slaving for it 24×7, it simply has no boundaries. No other creation of this universe can match its majestic trend, the activity it enjoys. Even the fastest of bullet trains, aircraft, rockets and space shuttles cannot outstrip it. Why, even H.G. Well's **Time Machine** would be a poor second in its back and forth speed.

Eternal knowledge lies not in the other world, but in the centre of consciousness. The human mind is the finest instrument which can be trained to realize the centre from which consciousness flows in various degrees and grades. It is the mind which shares joys and sorrows of others and contemplates weal and woe.

Mind is really two persons in one. One of these people is a little person one-ninth the size of the other, the big person. The active little person, the conscious mind likes to interfere, likes to be bossy, likes to control, and it has reason and logic and no memory. The big person, the subconscious has no reason and no logic but it has seat of memory.

---

1. Yatish Agarwal, *The World Within, Symptoms and Remedies of The Mind*, New Delhi: Raj Kamal Books, 2004.

Everything that has ever happened to a human, even things that happened before birth, are retained within the subconscious, and under suitable types of relaxations (like sleep, hypnosis, astral-travelling, etc.) that memory — dreams, regressions, distant projections, etc. — can be revived for consideration.

Conscious mind governs and directs our daily normal life, recording in the meantime every event and emotion that encounters its actions since childhood up to the present moment. Its duty and functioning is limited and restricted to the things that it already knows and its knowledge never exceeds the past (of present life) and the present. For this reason no conscious mind, however intelligent or superhuman it may be, can tell what will happen the next moment or what is going on next door. This restricted action of conscious mind is only manifested when this mind is awake. Once it becomes lulled or dormant as during sleep or in case of intoxication by drugs, it loses all control over the voluntary movements of the body; that is why when one goes to bed with a book or a cigarette and falls asleep the book or the cigarette drops without one's information. The brain being conquered by sleep loses its power over the grasping tendons of hand and thus it drops objects.

When the conscious mind is dormant, the subconscious mind starts to work. Unlike the conscious, the subconscious field of action is not limited, and that is the reason and main cause of vivid dreams and other manifestations experienced during the absence of the conscious mind.

Big doses of narcotic drugs, cocaine, opium, etc. give a magnificent illustration of the absence of the conscious mind which is stupefied and becomes inactive, leaving the field of action for the subconscious mind. The addicts often see whores, or fairies or whatever his heart desires — the hallucinations or illusions.

Some magnificent writers, poets, composers, and authors take drugs in order to awaken their subconscious minds which supply them with best ideas never attained in case of consciousness. Other methods to awaken subconscious are hypnotism, meditation and spiritualism.

The connection between the subconscious and conscious minds is only switched when one of them is dormant and the other awake. That is the reason why we dream of coming events or wish-fulfilment, etc. Both conscious and the subconscious mind are so connected with each other that the whole existence of any individual is governed and directed by both minds which work in shifts, the one replacing the other during its absence.

Our conscious mind is exactly like a camera lens with a thinking shutter, and the subconscious is like the negative where all photographed images get impressed. Dreams are positives, which are psychically developed.

A tranquil and purified mind can transcend the barrier of the sense world and reach the outermost frontiers of the world of time and space. It can glimpse what lies beyond the domain of senses. It gains extraordinary capabilities. It becomes all knowing; it can know all the events of the past, the present and the future — explaining the vividness of dreams one can have.

Broadly the human body has *three* invisible parts — the inner mind (subconscious mind) and the intellect (some call it unconscious mind) and lastly the soul. You need a perfect co-ordination among them. The outer mind (conscious mind) does not accept any suggestion easily. Characteristically it argues. However, the inner mind accepts every suggestion very easily and retains it for ever.

No one has seen the subconscious or unconscious mind, but most psychiatrists and psychologists conceive it with layers arranged like that in an onion. Ingenious labellers have named its divisions as preconscious, subconscious, underconscious, and supraconscious.

And yet, there is another view: the irradiated portion of our unconscious is subconscious. This irradiation has been done by our conscious knowingly as well as unknowingly, during this life since birth; and during our past lives, which comes with our soul as "past memory."

The irradiation has also been done by "universal consciousness," corresponding to our future and the future lives. It is like a video CD which gets recorded in view of our conscious as well as in our state of unawareness.

Just as a CD recorder registers whatever has been lasered onto it, in the same manner every experience we undergo, consciously or even unconsciously, is registered by the unconscious mind. The deepest layer in which the information is engraved, we call it "under-conscious" mind. The second layer of recording is not so deep. This is the subconscious level, where the data are in the process of transition and manifestation. The third layer or outermost layer of the storage on unconscious mind is in the process of fructification at the conscious mind level, and is called the preconscious. Thus our mind is: Conscious — Preconscious — Subconscious — Underconscious — Unconscious — Superconscious (Seed or Soul or Spirit or Roüh).

During dreams, a portion of the first few layers of the recording of the CD, i.e. preconscious to underconscious region get played, and the pictures are seen, which are due to us. A question arises here, why universal consciousness irradiates only a little portion — a part knowledge — a limited intelligence? The answer is simple. If you are supposed to know something, such as your future, your Higher Self will see to it that you receive that data. If, however, you are not supposed to be aware of certain future events, then no person, place, thing or technique (dreams, ESP, instinct, intuition, trance, etc.) will give you that information.

The fertile regions of unconscious mind are pullulating with nascent analogies, hidden likenesses, and the cloudy forms of things unknown to the conscious mind. But in dreams, most clouds form and dissolve again and again; only a few intuitions reach the stage of "seeding the cloud" which result in the formation of verbal drops; and cloud-bursts are a rarity — inventions guided by dreams.

However, dreaming state of the mind is the most powerful Hi-Fi radio and TV system when telepathic messages are readily received;

clairvoyant exposures and soul sorties are routine for some humans.

Superconscious state of mind includes simultaneous awareness of waking, dream and deep sleep states. There, simultaneous operation of the conscious, subconscious and unconscious sections of the mind results in single, enlightened state of consciousness in a perfectly integrated and relaxed personality. Those who have realized this state do not dream at all. They have one state of being which does not alter; waking and dreaming are alike for them, because they are continuously, sometimes quantumly, experiencing the spiritual state of superconsciousness — collective unconsciousness; illumination of the total mind or a state of Self-realization, *kaivalya*, *moksha* or *samadhi* or Liberation.

Thoughts and Dreams

The highest mystery that a human being wants to unveil is to know the nature of thought itself, the source from which the thinking process orginates, and ultimately, he wants to learn the true nature of his own self.

Thought is a ray of heavenly fire that penetrates every living thing on earth and unites in the closest bond all the various elements of the created world. A thought is a grosser form of free consciousness. The consciousness is the state of dynamic awareness. The awareness may be different at different levels — spiritual, intellectual, emotional, vital, and gross. Awareness at spiritual level is superconsciousness. Awareness at intellectual level is self-consciousness. Awareness at an emotional level may be called uniconsciouseness. Awareness at a vital level is subconsciousness, and awareness at the gross level is unconsciousness.

A thought passes through various layers of inner consciousness — conscious, subconscious, and unconscious, getting subtler and subtler, till it merges in the substratum in a vast ocean of thought-free pure awareness. It is from this source that the thought had arisen in seed form and achieved its final evolutionary form at the conscious level; during its outward journey it had gathered various components of knowledge in the form of memory, ideas, symbols, beliefs and fantasies.

Thoughts are the mental images that pop up in our minds. Feelings or emotions occur when we react to these thoughts. Thoughts during the sleep may result in dreams.

While you are awake, there are many things you see, smell, taste, touch and feel in a single day. All this supplies food for thought, reminiscence, and speculation during the day. It is no different while we are asleep; when you do not see, your sense organs continue to bring you sense of taste and feelings of temperature, pressure, pain, position, etc. If you have eaten something which does not agree with your appetite, your stomach-ache will report this to the brain, which will supply food for thought in your dream life. During dreaming, the codes of disciplined reasoning are suspended. Therefore, thoughts modulated by their own emotional gravity, drift in "lawless" fashion in dreams and in riveries.

Thoughts form mental pictures on our inner screens. Our entire thought process and dreams are in fact a series of photographic images which flow through the mind. We produce and direct these pictures.

The waves which form these pictures get originated in our brain. Our brain is coupled with mind and its components: conscious, sub-conscious, unconscious, superconscious; as well as thought process. The brain's activity is reflected by the waves it generates. The main waves are given in Table II; besides there is a series of brain waves, which are of lesser significance.

In dreams, visual explorations and mental explorations are actually indistinguishable. The dream images, thought images, and visualization experiences are intermingled in case of intellectuals and creative persons. The creative act, insofar as it depends on unconscious resources, presupposes a relaxing of the controls and regression to modes of ideation which are indifferent to the rules of verbal logic. The unconscious is unperturbed by contradiction and is untouched by the dogmas and taboos of so-called common sense.

Thinking is a continuous oscillation between conscious and unconscious processes — consciousness and unconsciousness being

Table II — EEG Waves

S. No.	Wave Pattern	Freq-uency Hz	Associated Mind	State of Consci-ousness	State of Mind	Orient-ation of Mind	Realm of Experience	Electric Potential - micro Volts	Magnetic Field - Tesla	Stimu-lative Essence	Experi-ences of
1.	Beta-β	40-14	Conscious	Awareness	Active Thinking	Extroversion Anxiety Worry Logic Reasoning	Sensory awareness External knowledge	5-10	$\sim 2.5 \times \sim 10^{-13}$	Jasmine Rosemary Cardamom	Relative-World
2.	Alfa-∝	14-8	Sub-conscious	Drow-siness	Relaxed Medi-tative	Pre-hypnotic Day-dreaming Reverie	Relaxation Conscious-dreaming archetypal-imagery	50	$\sim 2.0 \times \sim 10^{-12}$	Lavender Melissa Chamo-mile	World within (Mental Realm)
3.	Theta-θ	8-4	Under-conscious Tumescent-uncon-scious	Dream-ing-sleep unaware	Restfull Expan-sive	Dreaming ESP Visions Creativity	Dreams, Release of emotions, Suppressed fears and desires, OOBEs	10	$\sim 5 \times \sim 10^{-5}$ *	Neroli	World underneath (the conscious)
4.	Delta-δ	4-0	Unconsc-ious	Sound-sleep	Totally unaware	Dreamless-sleep Sleep of new borns	Awakening of instincts Primitive-drives NDEs	20-200	—	Rose Lilac Violet	World-Reality

*the theta wave magnetic field corresponds to the Earth's magnetic pulsation of 0.5 gauss (5×10^{-5} Tesla) at 7.5 Hz; the magnetic field drops as the frequency rises.

like warp and weft. True picture-strip thinking is confined to manifestations of the unconscious — the dreams, the hypnogogic half-dreams, the psychotics hallucinations, the artist's visions.

The dream as remembered and reported is not the "real thing" at all, but a distorted substitute, "which, by calling up other substitute-ideas, provide us with a means of approaching the thought proper, of bringing into consciousness the unconscious thoughts underlying the dream," said Freud in 1920.

> Mind is the great lever of all things; human thought is the process by which human ends are ultimately answered. — *Daniel Webster*

Thinking in the past is remembering; thinking in the present is mainly problem solving; and thinking in the future is anticipating — the three processes, which result in dreams. A.B. Alcott said, "Thought means life, since those who do not think do not live in any high or real sense. Thinking makes the man."

Finally, many of our day thoughts are day dreams, just as many of our night dreams are night thoughts.

Creativity and Dreams

In dreams the mind is led forward into ever widening thought and action. In turn dreams have intellectually challenging effects necessary for creativity.

The creative act[2] is not an act of creating something out of nothing; it uncovers, selects, reshuffles, combines, and synthesizes already existing facts, ideas, faculties, and skills. The more familiar the parts, the more striking the new whole. Man's knowledge of the changes of the tides and the phases of the moon is as old as his observation that apples fall to the earth when they are ripe. Yet the combination of these and other equally familiar data in Newton's theory of gravity changed mankind's outlook on the world.

Celebrated discoveries are made by mainly two processes: the

---

2. Arthur Koestler, *The Act of Creation*, London: Pan Books Ltd., 1977.

first apparantly due to conscious logical reasoning aided by chance; the second by classic intervention of the unconscious.

Creativity is an intellectual exercise, a feat of mental acrobatics, which is sublimated in the unconscious. The unconscious gives rise to the mysterious inspirations and sudden flashes of insight, which aid the onset of the creativity.

Discovery consists in seeing an analogy which nobody had seen before. The analogy may strike in more rational fashion, or in more dramatic and bizarre style. At the very start of our enquiry we hit on a pattern — the discovery that a playful or *l'art pour l'art* technique provides an unexpected clue to problems in a quite different field — which is one of the leitmotifs in the history of science.

Creativity strikes the prepared mind. With searching mind, the creative stress results from the blocked situation which keeps the problem on the agenda even while the beam of consciousness keeps drifting to quite other scenarios. Without this constant pressure, the favourable chance — constellation would have passed unnoticed — and joined the legion of man's missed opportunities for a creative departure from the stale habits of thought which numb his mental powers.

The history of scientific discoveries suggests, outwittingly, that some of the researchers and investigators got the clues for their inventions and revelations in their sleeps or in the state of insomania.

Further review of exemplary inventions explains a puzzling but recurrent phenomenon in the history of science: that the same discovery is made, more or less at same time, by two or more people; and it may also help to explain the independent development of the same techniques and similar styles of art in different cultures.

Primitive man of the stone age appears to have utilized hardly 1 per cent of his brain capacity, his activities being minimal for survival and fecundity. The utilization of brain potential increased considerably through the Bronze and Copper ages till the Iron age. In this Silicon age he is able to use nearly 10 to 15 per cent of his brain capacity.

Higher utilization of the brain potential up to 25 per cent can open up the door to pure imagination and intuition — a faculty of mind where the reason and logic are transcended and unexpected and original observations are arrived at a flash.

Max Planck, the father of Quantum Theory, wrote in his autobiography that the pioneer scientist must have "a vivid intuitive imagination for new ideas not generated by deduction, but by artistically creative imagination."

When the utilization of brain capacity approaches 50 per cent, as it happens in dreams, it leads to insight, wherein the full knowledge in any field of activity flashes across the mind bypassing the laborious process of logical ratiocination. In the case of one seized with the existing problems, intuition is a brief communion with cosmic intelligence, while insight represents a more complete inmersion in Cosmic Creation.

In the dreams the codes of logical reasoning are suspended, so "thinking aside" is a temporary liberation from the tyranny of over-precise verbal concepts, of the axioms and prejudices engrained in the very texture of specialized ways of thought. It allows the mind to discard the straitjacket of habit, to shrug off apparent contradictions, to un-learn and forget — and to acquire, in exchange, a greater fluidity, versatility and gullibility. This rebellion against constraints which are necessary to maintain the order and discipline of conventional thought, but an impediment to creative leap, is symptomatic both of genius and the crank; what distinguishes them is the intuitive guidance which only the former enjoys.

Dreaming, in the literal and metaphorical sense, seems to be an essential part of psychic metabolism — as essential as its counterpart, the formation and automatization of habits. Without this daily dip into the ancient sources of mental life, we would probably all become desiccated automata. And without the more spectacular exploratory dives of the creative individual, there would be no science and no art.

The source of creativity is in dreams, and the symbol of creativity is the magic wand which Moses used to make water come out of the rock; its reverse is the faulty yardstick which turns everything it touches into dust.

So the creative dream and our conditioned consciousness' dance will become apparent in the ultimate outcome of our creative endeavour, which will be an intelligent well-written essay that respects both the unconscious source of the ideas and our accumulated knowledge, experience and judgement on the subject.

Psychic Attacks and Dreams

The psychic attacks, insults, and evil spirits are responsible for a barrage of bad luck, physical ailments, accidents and even neuroses. However, key symptom of such an assault is a series of emotionally charged mental conflicts (ECMCs). Dreams during REM phase of sleep account for about 10 per cent of such attacks, though this percentage figure is yet to be statistically averaged out.

A sensitive, intuitive, creative and mentally docile person may expose himself/herself to such an abuse by coming in contact or closeness to such a source/perpetrator but a normal person is also susceptible to the source by syncronization and resonance of brain-waves telepathically while conscious or dreaming.

Many alleged psychic attacks are reported by paranoid, schizophrenics, hysteronics, and patients with severe cases of mood swings, such as bipolars (formerly called maniac-depressives). But, conventional medicine and psychotherapy have been ineffective with the true psychic attack victims. Physicians are also stumped, since all of their traditional tests come out negative.

Some of the remedial measures include aura manipulations, aura shielding, hypnotic-life-regression, dream-analysis-psychiatry, and superconscious-mind-tap. For evacuating the unwanted soul/spirits, shamanic rituals and white magic are solutions. Facing the invading spirit/souls during lucid-dreaming and during hypno-meditation-trance is a perfect formulation for avoiding psychic attacks and abrasions.

Dr Bruce Goldberg, a clinical hypnotist from California, U.S.A.

has studied and treated successfully many subjects who were victims of the psychic attacks and evil spirits.[3]

Diseases and Dreams

We live at least two existences, conscious and unconscious. Our health and wholeness are contigent upon the degree of relatedness between these two aspects of existence. When these two disconnect, another bridge appears to connect them: this bridge is a symbol. It may appear in a dream, a fantasy, or relationship; as enchantment with certain myths or a fairy tale; or as a medical or psychiatric illness. When understood in a symbolic context, these phenomena reconnect us with our inner unconscious life and re-establish health, healing, and wholeness.

In dreaming, the *Brihadaranyaka Upanishad** observes, we leave one world and enter another. "In that dream world there are no chariots, no animals to draw them, no roads to ride on, but one makes chariots and animals and roads oneself from the impressions of past experience." And then the leap of insight: "Everyone experiences this, but no one knows the experiencer." What is same in both the worlds, the observer both of waking experience and of dreams? It cannot be the body, for in dreams it detaches itself from the body and senses and creates its own experiences — experiences which can be as real, in terms of physiological reactions, as those of waking life. "When a man dreams that he is being killed or chased by an elephant, or that he is falling into a well, he experiences the same fear that he would experience in the waking state": his heart races, blood pressure rises, stress hormones pour into the body, just as if the event was real. Dream and waking are made of same stuff, and as far as the nervous system is concerned — the root of most diseases.

We know what forces can buffet us in the dream world, and that is only the foothills of the dark ranges of mind, where fear, passion egotism, and desire so easily sweep aside the will. One of Hopkins'

3. Bruce Goldberg, *Self-defence against Psychic Attacks and Evil Spirits*, New Delhi: Pustak Mahal, 1999.

* Upanishad is a mystical text given by the illumined seers, attached to the end of one of the four Vedas.

"dark sonnets" hints at the danger of these realms:

O the mind, mind has mountains;
cliffs of fall, frightful, sheer, non-man-fathomed.
Hold them cheap.
May, who never hung there . . . ,
which becomes the fount of psychosomatic diseases.

Dreaming, however, is probably the normal mechanism for adjusting **reach-back** (It is defined as that period of time during which an impending event begins to have an independent influence on the individual's behaviour. It is most dramatically seen in people with phobias, whose whole functioning may be disturbed for days ahead at the prospect of getting into a feared situation.) and **after-burn** (it is defined as that period of time during which a past event has an independent disturbing influence on the individual's behaviour for an appreciable period). Since sedatives such as barbiturates reduce the amount of REM dream sleep in favour of other stages of sleep, they do not encourage the assimilation of reach-back and after-burn; the effect may be to "deposit" the unassimilated overlap in some part of the body, leading to a "psychosomatic" disorder. That, however, may sometimes be preferable to the effects of prolonged and extensive insomnia.

A man who is deaf from an early stage (age), hears no sound in his dreams. Likewise blind people dream a good deal, mostly of hearing, touch and smell.

Persistent or recurring dreams can be traced almost invariably, to some physical (like diseases, ambient noises, etc.) or psychological (perturbed mind) cause and as a rule have no futuristic significance. However, a dream that recurs only two or three times needs to be microscoped. And, the healthy dreams occurring a couple of times are indication of vitality and virility.

Dreams of being shot through the chest or crushed can often point to problems with the cardiovascular system or lungs. Chest problems result in dreams where you will be fighting for breath.

Houses on fire can often point to ulcers or indigestion. Fever may give rise to dreams of fire, liver problems lead to yellow or green coloured fluids in the dreams. Jaundice provides dreams of nasty taste in the mouth, thirst, heat and hot deserts.

Urinary problems lead to images of water, overflowing river, canal; lake brimming with water.

Hysterical persons dream of snakes, black cats and similar creatures.

Freud has suggested that anxiety nightmares, culminating in a sudden, terrifying awakening, are often prevalent in dreamers with diseases of the heart; while those with lung diseases are prone to dreams of suffocation, crowding or fleeing. Indigestion may as well lead to nightmares.

Literally a nightmare was a spirit, according to the nineteenth century books. The Anglo-Saxon word "mare" meant an evil spirit or monster that came during the night and sat on the chests of sleeping people. It stopped their breathing, creating bad dreams and an oppresive feeling. In the Middle Ages they were call night-hags. Then Freud got hold of them, and the nightmares were never the same again.

Of all dreams, nightmares need an express attention. The four solutions are:

1. Liberal dose of Vitamin B_1 (Thiamine hydrochloride) will give relief from nightmares — 40 mgs a day in two doses for 5 to 10 days.
2. Flowers of carnation by the bedside will keep nightmares away.
3. A few drops of Eucalyptus oil in a bowl of water will ease nightmares and the disturbed sleep.
4. Coral gem hung on the bedpost will prevent nightmares.

Another interesting method of having control over nightmares has been elucidated by Deepa Kodical:[4] "Early in life, when I was

4. Deepa Kodikal, *A Journey Within the Self: A Diary of Yogic Experiences*, New Delhi: Viva Book Private Ltd., 2006, p. xxvii.

eight or ten, I realized that I could direct my dreams. Ordinary dreams or nice dreams were, of course, a pleasure to have; but during nightmares, of which I had a generous quota, the gift of directed "propulsion" acted like an invincible armour against any fear. I was a timid child and was always petrified at night. In my nightmares, I would be perpetually followed by a band of gypsies, or find a big feline stalking me or trying to enter the house, or I would have an encounter with ghosts. Haunted thus repeatedly, one day I mentioned to my mother that I was scared at nights. An off-hand remark by her, to make light of my fright and to reassure me, changed my life altogether. She said, "There is nothing to be scared of. It is your dream. Only you can see those creatures. They can't see you."

> I was stunned. How true, I thought. If the creatures peopling my dreams cannot see me, then if I were to stand still where I was, they would bypass me. I would be safe! With a herculean effort of will, I put this to the test at night, in the nightmare that followed. I was being followed by the same band of gypsies. With all the courage I could gather, I stood at my ground and did not flee as I normally did. And, to my utter disbelief, I saw the band moving on from either side of me oblivious of me. I was invisible to them. They could not see me, they could not feel me, and what's more, they walked through me as if I was not there. I stood trembling in the middle of the road for a long while digesting this incredible occurrence.
>
> Now I was my own master. Fully armed thus, nightmares thereafter became, after the initial fright and slight uncertainty, a challenge from which I would come out unscathed.
>
> From hereon, it was only a matter of time before I concluded that I could do all sorts of impossible things in a dream. So, when the gypsies arrived next, instead of willing myself invisible, I jumped like a blob of flubber and landed on a branch high up a tree. Now nightmares were fun. Any time the gypsies or the tiger or the lion appeared, I would become invisible or become a piece of flubber or would just take off on a sortie. Now dreams became flights of fantasy.

Jonas Salk said it best when he wrote: "I have had dreams and I have had nightmares, I overcame the nightmares because of my dreams." Dare to dust off your dreams. Start to revere life and celebrate all its wonders. Awaken yourself to the power of your own mind to make things happen. Once you do, the universe will conspire with you to work magic in your life, according to the Monk, who sold his Ferrari.[5]

A dream represents the hidden fulfilment of unconscious wishes, which, when repressed, produce a chain of psychic consequences, frequently disastrous. Dream or nightmare, we have to live our experience as it is, and we have to live it wide awake. We live in a world which is penetrated through and through by science, and which is both whole and real. We cannot turn the experience into a game simply by taking sides. What we can do is to sleep well (sound sleep) either by taking sleeping pills (as an honest, middle class man does) or by consuming alcohol (as corrupt or high profile people do) or by practising meditation, so as not to have dreams remembered. The best way is: "Do not sleep on your back. That is wrong posture — results in bad dreams. It interferes with the process of natural digestion, puts pressure over kidneys. For men that is the posture that is most favourable for wet dreams. Lie on your left."

There is a point at which you wake up fresh, the body feels quiet. Do not go to bed again. You will sink into anxiety, inertia and lethargy that will swollow your freshness, pull down your consciousness, cause a surge of confused dreams. And, if you have had an interesting dream, try to trace it back from the point you woke up. That may help you in the process of healing.

Drugs and Dreams

A number of drugs affect our sleep, consequently exerting a powerful influence on dreams. For example, alcohol consumption leads to disturbing dreams of reptiles if taken in excess. Opium dreams are

---

5. Robins S. Sharma, *The Monk Who Sold His Ferrari – A Fable about fulfilling your Dreams and Reaching Your Destiny*, Mumbai: Jaico Publishing House, 2005, p. 49.

more voluptuous and grandiose. Hashish induces horrible nightmares, and sometimes homicidal mania. The fumes of carbon-bisulphide induces nightmares in which the sleeper leaps over precipices, or is brutally murdered.

Barbiturates, tranquilizers and alcohol all produce abnormalities in dreaming and interfere with the normal dream process of releasing repressed aggressions and hostilities, resulting in anxiety, irritability and paranoia.

The paranoia caused by dreams or conscious circumstances can be easily brought under control by moderate doses (about 1 mg each night before going to sleep, for fifteen days) of "Trifluoperazine Hydrochloride." Liberal doses of Vitamin B_1 (Thiamine hydrochloride) will give relief from nightmares.

The dreams and nightmares may result in Schizophrenia in the old persons, which may be treated with Chlorpromazine (Largactil), Alprazolam (Alprax), Thioridazine (Melleril) and Pimozide (Orap). However, a competent doctor need to be consulted.

Sleeping pills are no remedy for bad dreams and sleeplessness. They are habit forming and become less effective when taken continuously. They lower the I.Q. level, dull the brain and creativity, and can prove fatal if taken in excess and before or after alcohol.

Instances of persons taking an overdose of sleeping pills with fatal results are quite frequent. Insomnia deprives a person of mental rest and thereby interferes with his activities in the daytime which in turn affects the dreaming. An Ayurvedic remedy is take a pinch of nutmeg powder at the time of going to bed — this is the best solution.

Races and Dreams

Dreams are as individual as the people who have them. The Romans and Greeks believed that dreams were the warnings of future happenings, and the Egyptians thought the gods spoke through dreams, giving rise to dream-related superstitions. The Hebrews thought that dreams were very important, and offen carried out their affairs according to the dictates of a dream. By 1400s it was believed that "dreams go by contraries"— whatever you dreamed meant the exact opposite.

Edwin Radford, in his *Encyclopaedia of Superstitions* (1949), gathers up a list of what many dreams are supposed to mean:

- Dreams of sickness means marriage among young peoples.
- Dreams of angels indicate happiness coming quite soon.
- To have dreamed of standing before an altar implies sorrow and misfortune.
- Dream of being angry with someone special and that person will turn out to be your best friend.
- Dreaming of fishing mean that for each fish you catch, a friend will die soon.
- Dreams of dancing indicate good fortune is coming.
- Dreams that you've gone bald and you'll lose friends or property.
- A dream of a wedding means death.
- Dreams of bees or bee stings are very bad luck.
- Dream of fruit out of season and you will wake up in tears.
- Dream of marriage and birds always mean death and illness.

The Aborigines of Australia accord huge importance to the process of dreaming and listening to communications for health and wealth. The Naskapi Indians of Labrador Peninsula in Canada rely on dreams in their everyday life.

It has been seen that the dreams are based upon your racial, cultural and social conditioning. Dreams are based also on your professional associations. Dreams may be secular or otherwise, depending upon your previous lives and present religious or political alignment.

The Dream Applications

A dream is a dynamic expression of forces which, though repressed are struggling to regain a place in consciousness. Dream seems to be a beautiful illustration of the mechanism by which instinctual tendencies in conflict with ego are manifested.

Depravity does not lie in the nature of dreams; in fact, you know that there are dreams which can be recognized as gratifying justifiable desires; and urgent bodily needs. It is true that there is no distortion in these dreams; they care to perform their function without offending the aesthetic tendencies of the ego.

Dream researchers seem to be divided into two classes — those who are trying to evolve a system of using dreams for increasing a person's effectiveness and productivity and those who continue to treat dreams as a form of mysticism.

Jewish mysticism, one of the oldest and most intriguing spiritual systems, insists that dreams offer us a key avenue for self-exploration and a path to greater wisdom concerning the cosmos. The Kabbalah (from the Hebrew root-word meaning "to receive"), considers dreams of great significance for everyday life.

Lichtenberg, a hunch-backed genius, satirical writer, and professor of physics at Goettingen, Germany, regarded dreams as a means to self-knowledge.

Dreams of prophetic or telepathic nature have been recorded, wherein dreamers have "witnessed" accidents, "read" headlines pertaining to disasters or have been "told" the name of a horse that turned out to be the winner. These are often few and far between to be judged accurately, but they constitute an intriguing phase of dream experience.

Dreams have also helped in the psychological healing process — while innermost recesses of mind give expression to shocks, fears, ailments and impeding catastrophes. Dreams have also resulted in mental instabilities.

Dreams analysed in proper perspective can be part of solution search and of decision-making processes.

It is the mind which projects the dream and the soul which witnesses it. The mind is the "divine display" for the soul, and it is mind which sees, which hears, which smells, which tastes, which feels a touch of an action in the past, present, or future. Therefore, dreams serve one of the following purposes:

1. To presage future events.
2. To disclose unknown secrets.
3. To provide different options for unsolved problems.
4. To boost creativity.
5. To release internal tensions and stresses.
6. To enjoy unknown blisses in privacy.

The Dreamer

Everybody dreams, but by "Dreamer" what we understand is "Master Dreamer," which expatiated further, is "Mister or Miss or Missis Dreamer." S/he is a character who is fond of dreams, and always or invariably, has vivid dreams. The dreamer has her/his own views about the meaning of dreams. S/he can provide correct interpretation of dreams. It takes her/him considerable time during waking hours to think over and solve dreams; and always looks thoughtful and absent-minded.

S/he could be easily recognized from her/his small head and big dull face which grows wider at the temples and narrow at the forehead which protrudes. Her/his ears are small, her/his hairs are soft, smooth and bright; her/his eyes are big, bright and liable to goitre; her/his eyebrows, are thick and often meet above the nose which is small, narrow and turned upwards at the base. Her/his lips are big, the lower one protruding a little bit. Her/his chin is very thick and composed of two- or threefolds which hide her/his neck. The dreamer's shoulders are narrow and her/his chest is likewise narrow and fat and produces a thin voice like that of children.

Astrologically as understood in the West, the dreamer may have Moon as a ruling luminary, and/or other luminary Sun posited in aquarian zodiac.

On his/her palm the mount of Luna (moon) is of medium size and flabby abdominous stature. The head line will be drooping towards this mount of moon. They will have clear line of Instinct or Intuition or what is called as the sixth sense which enables persons to predict coming events. Dreams of such persons are very vivid and they make their calculations upon such dreams. They are also fond of occult sciences especially hypnotism and spiritualism, and awful fancies.

The "dreamer" has long, slender, pointed fingers; thin, elongated palm. S/he has prominent mounts of Moon, Venus and sometimes Saturn (if the dreams are tinged with sadness). The very drooping line of Head and a line of "Intuition," often islanded at the start. A cross close to the line of the sun represents religious ecstasy.

The dreamer's spectrum is covered by an artist at one end and a jester on the other. The artist is an inspired dreamer — a solitary figure, eccentric, impractical, selfish, and quixotic. The Jester (Falstaff) spurns the dreamer. In between these antagonistic types once stood the Sage (or Shaman) who combined the qualitities of both: a sagacious dreamer with his head in the clouds and his feet on the solid earth. Close to him today, stands a Scientist — the dry, dull, diligent, pedantic, peerish, petulant, scholarly book-worm, uninspired and with his crabbed little world.

The "Orient" has been the cradle of the human race for ages, and all the vicissitudes of fortune are there: kingdoms succeeding kingdoms; empires succeeding empires; human power, glory, and wealth, all rolling down there — a Golgotha of power and learning. No wonder the "Oriental" looks with contempt upon the things of this world and naturally wants to see something that changeth not, something which dieth not, something which in the midst of this world of misery and death is eternal, blissful, undying — a fount of dreams.

The "Oriental" is a visionary, is a born dreamer. The ripples of the waterfalls, the songs of the birds, the beauties of the sun and moon and stars and the whole earth, are pleasant enough; but they are not sufficient for the Oriental. He wants to dream a dream beyond. He wants to go beyond. He wants to go beyond the present. The present, as it were, is nothing to him. He aspires to be the dreamer.

4

Dream Philosophies

A DREAM takes its position in concatenation of our psychic activities as a link of definite importance and value. During last 120 years, five major schools of philosophy got propounded by psychologists to unveil the very complicated task of explaining the meaning and purpose of dreams and dreaming. They are:

1. Sigmund Freud (1856-1939) School.
2. Carl Gustav Jung (1875-1961) School.
3. Calvin Stanley Hall School.
4. Fritz Perls School.
5. Joseph Banks Rhine School.

Besides the above five schools, we have:

6. Buddhist Thinking, and
7. Current Thinking.

All of these are briefly discussed below.

Freud School

Sigmund Freud believed that one's unconscious and repressed hopes, fears, frustrations, wishes and desires will come through and appear in one's dream life. There are many shameful and unconscious thoughts that have been repressed in an individual's life, but which will break into his/her conscious when his/her critical faculties are relaxed. The dream content will be disguised by what Freud calls the "dream censor" in order to make it acceptable to the individual's ego.

A dream is a dynamic expression of forces which, though repressed, are struggling to regain a place in consciousness. The dream seemed to be a beautiful illustration of the mechanism by which instinctual tendencies in conflict with the ego are manifested.

According to Freud, dreams are caused by wishes — the strong wishes. As conscious wishes are seldom intense enough to produce a dream, it is the unconscious infantile wishes, which possess a quantum of energy and can utilize it to reinforce a conscious wish that has some association of ideas with them. The dream is then an imaginary fulfilment of the wish relieving the mind and soothing the nervous system. The unconscious wishes are selfish, and the dreams are also egoistic, and if the dreamer does not appear imaged in his own person, he is present as something or somebody else.

The dream, wrote Freud, neglects in the most conspicuous manner the logical category of opposition and contradiction. The concept "No" does not seem to exist in the dream. It likes to compress opposites into a unity, or to represent them as one. It takes the further liberty of representing any given entity by its emotional opposite, so that a priori one never knows whether a reversible entity is thought of in the dream with a "plus or minus sign."

In 1900, with the publication of *The Interpretation of Dreams*, Sigmund Freud agreed that dreams were the "royal road" to the unconscious; that they revealed in disguised form the deepest elements of an individual's inner life. In 1920, Freud wrote, "Desires which we believe alien to human nature show themselves powerful enough to give rise to dream."

Freud found and argued that dreams do really possess a meaning, and are by no means the expression of a disintegrated cerebral activity, as the writers on the subject would have us believe. The dream is not comparable to the irregular sounds of a musical instrument, which, instead of being played by the hand of a musician, is struck by some external force; the dream is not meaningless, not absurd, does not presuppose that one part of our store of ideas is dormant while another part begins to awake. It is a perfectly valid psychic phenomenon, actually a wish-fulfilment; it may be enrolled in the continuity of the intelligible psychic activities of the waking state; it is built up by a highly complicated intellectual activity.

Sigmund Freud (1856-1939) Austrian physician, neurologist, and founder of psychoanalysis. He was born in Freiberg on 6 May 1856, and was educated at Vienna University, where he remained for most of his life.

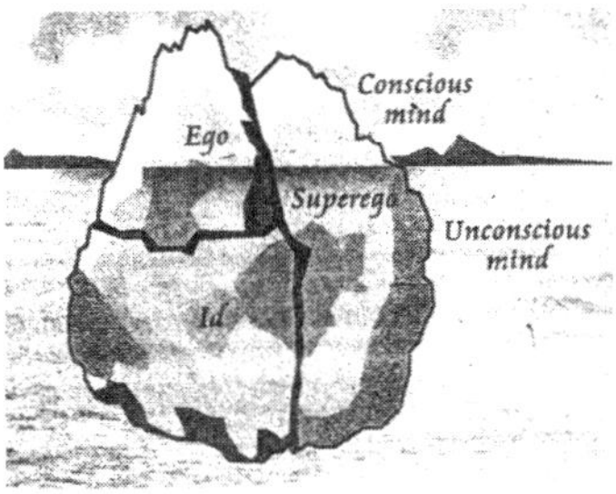

Freud's psychoanalytic theory. The mind is like an iceberg. The tip above the water represents consciousness, and the vast region below the surface symbolizes the unconscious mind.

Jung School

Carl G. Jung has said that the unconscious is a kind of repository for dream images, both archetypal and otherwise, with the perhaps mistaken belief that it is somewhat finite. When we recognize that the unconscious is in fact infinite, though accessible to us, dreams achieve their proper place in the hierarchy of awareness, as a way of accessing that limitless source of information — each of us is plugged into a "collective unconscious" — an underground storehouse of memories through which minds can communicate.

In dreams there is a sense of temporal and spatial infinity, speed and an extension of movement. They are also distinguished by symbols of telluric (i.e. magical) and astrological significance, and lunar as well as solar signs, and also changes in the proportions of the body. Therefore, understand dream images symbolically, that is, do not take them literally but find a hidden meaning. They emanate from an unknown part of the psyche and may prepare the dreamer for the events of the following days.

Jung ascertained that anima and animus help the individual to develop a better understanding of the opposite sex. In fact, the archetype, the anima, is the hidden female in every man and the animus is the hidden male in every woman. Obviously the animus characterizes male behaviour, that is aggressiveness, cruelty, obstinacy, etc. while the anima describes kindness, politeness, generosity, and such like. The presence of anima in a man makes him less aggressive and generous person, while animus in a woman makes her bold enough and self-assured. The anima appears in a man's dream in the form of a woman with no face or strange face. Also the animus in a woman's dream appears in the form of a man with strange characters.

Hall School

Calvin S. Hall has suggested that there is continuity between waking thought and dream content. In other words, dreams reflected waking concerns, interests, and emotional focus. This led him to divide dream content into several categories: characters, emotions, interactions, misfortunes, objects and settings. He discovered that dreams express conceptions of family members, friends, social environment and self. He has emphasized the usefulness of keeping a dream diary and the necessity of continually looking at wider context of dreams.

Carl Gustav Jung (1875-1961) was a psychiatrist by profession but a psychic by nature.

1909: Pioneers of psychoanalysis assembled at the Clark University, USA. Top row: (left to right) A.A. Brill, Ernest Jones, and Sandor Ferenczi; and bottom row: Sigmund Freud, C. Stanley Hall, and Carl Gustav Jung.

Perls School

Fritz Perls believed that the dreams needed no interpretation; dreams should be brought back to life and acted out in the present.

He held that all the details of the dream had relevance, for every person, for everything and for every mood. By becoming each of these and setting up encounters between them, the dreamer could come to a deeper understanding of himself as a "real" personality. He recognized that in the dream state and by understanding the dreams we could integrate opposing forces within our self.

It is fair then to say that this method does not interpret dreams — that is, we do not say that the dream means such and such — but that the dream has given us a particular insight into ourselves, which we can use in our daily lives.

Rhine School

Joseph Banks Rhine, a First World War veteran and a botany student who became intrigued by para-psychology, won a place at the newly-created department of psychology at Duke University, North Carolina, U.S.A. In 1920, Rhine described an interesting situation — What use would the warnings in dreams (also through extra-sensory-perceptions, ESP) be if one could not take the clue and change the eventuality? For example, if a person sees in a dream that the train in which s/he is going to travel the next week has met with an accident, can s/he change her/his destiny? The answer to this question is that those people, who are destined to live, will heed the warning and will not travel in the train. Others will not heed the warning: they will travel and die, in accordance with their destiny. So the destiny is unchangeable, but dreams bring about the fulfilment of the destinies of each and every person.

All those who are destined to survive a catastrophe or an accident shall heed to a warning given by dreams; to their instincts or superstitious belief or vision; and listen to a telepathic message given by their well-wishers, or to any other precognitive signal. Perhaps nature keeps reshuffling the plans of human beings, according to various requirements. What can be changed and what cannot be changed in one's destiny is a debatable question — destiny, fate, coincidence, chance, probabitity . . . !

J.B. Rhine studied ESP extensively.
Waking, it is ESP; while sleeping it is dream.

Buddhist School

Buddhist thoughts suggest that the dreams arise due to mental activity of imagination. Whenever an idea is generated in our mind it is stored in our subconscious and when we sleep that idea or chain of ideas get displayed over the screen of our mind. It happens because at that time all our scenes get connected with the outer world and our heart takes the charge in place of our head.

Moreover, according to Buddhist savants, those who are true saints and/or monks, do not have dreams as their heads and hearts are in stable harmony and they need not look for material gains. However, there is a little contradiction here, as such persons are claimed to have the capability to see their past and future through dreams and other psychic telescopes. Nevertheless, dreams seem to be the keys to our mental faculties.

Current Philosophy

The world view is "Dreams are images through which the unconscious communicates with our conscious." Surrealists agree that understanding of one's dreams leads to independence from the criticism of others and from habitual self-assessment — one becomes aware of new dimensions and evolved perceptions. Therefore, one should regularly record events of daily life, and the dreams seen, so that s/he can correlate the dreams with daily happenings and get guidance from them. Changing perceptions of time and space by mind during sleep, should be heeded. One may consult various books available in the market, but it is desirable to make one's own directory of dreams eventually, for futurologistics. In due course one may find that the mind expresses itself over and over again through symbols, which are very personal to the dreamer. One may come to know that dreams occur at different levels and may begin to understand them directly and clearly.

Dreams are never identical, and if they may have similarities, their eventuation will be reflective of the dreamer's personality and environments.

Just an overview, an artist carves out the image of God which he saw hidden in a piece of wood. A comedian discovers that he has known the god from the plum-tree. A scientist, or better to say a sage, sees the god in a grain of sand — Laplace regarded it as the ultimate aim of science to demonstrate from a single grain of sand the "mechanics of the whole universe"; Hindu saints do claim *kan kan mein bhagwan hain*; Kepler, contemplating a snow-crystal (microcosmic architecture) melting on his always sweaty palm, saw in it the harmony of the spheres (planets) reflected in miniature. A dreamer may catch his breath and wax equally lyrical: "How strange — how beautiful — how clever is nature," etc.

Think of what the world owes to our forefathers' dream of democracy. That mighty dream which crumbled thrones and toppled monarchies in the past has gone on increasing in vividness and strength until today mankind is actually talking of a World Republic.

5

Dream Types

DREAMS can be creative, destructive, dull, entertaining, exciting, frightening, funny, futuristic, oracular, realistic, repetitive, reportive, suggestive, symbolic, etc. The dreams, therefore need to be categorized for the purpose of illustration.

Dreams can be classified in a variety of ways, such as:

1. Natural,
2. Induced.

Further, the induced dreams can be categorized as: on demand and recreated.

Another way of classification can be:

1. Time-based
2. Content-oriented

These can further be broken into different ways:

1. Future-related
   - (i) Solutions to pending problems
   - (ii) Action to be taken
   - (iii) Premonitions, foreshadows, prophetics, etc.
   - (iv) Progressionistic — Future births and lives
2. Present-goings
   - (i) Review of day's work
   - (ii) Anxieties and fears
   - (iii) Thought undulations

(iv) Beliefs, superstitions.

3. Past happenings

   (i) Previous events

   (ii) Regressionistic — Previous births and lives

and, all of these may overlap each other as our mind can reach all the shores of cosmic consciousness. Friedrich Hebbell, who was a dedicated student of dream problems, stated that "In dreams fantasy gets even with the shameless imp, Reason." And Cicero, the Roman statesman and author (106–43 BCE), wrote almost two thousand years ago, "Nothing can be so silly, so impossible, or so unnatural that it cannot happen in a dream." Therefore, forgetting about vividness, dreams will be discussed briefly under the following listing:

1. Anxiety Dreams
2. Archetypal and Symbolic Dreams
3. Daydreams
4. Lucid Dreams
5. On-demand Dreams
6. Prodromal Dreams
7. Recreated Dreams
8. Visitation Dreams
9. Astral Travelling Dreams
10. Implanted Dreams

All dreams have a definite order, form and meaning. Each person's dream resonates his attitude, behavioural patterns, work worries, etc. For example, it has been noted that the computer expert's or management executive's dream is a structured format; while artists, musicians and others tend to be free in their dreams. A nuclear physics student has been heard shouting in the sleep "Neutron is coming up, stop it there." However, this could also be due to the difference in the forms of expression while recalling dreams.

Anxiety Dreams

When we do not feel that we have control of what is happening, then anxiety results. During this phase of the life the dreams are replays of our niggling anxieties. An intellectual has correctly described such dreams. Khushwant Singh[1] says,

> I dream a lot at night and during my afternoon siesta. Much as I try I can make no sense out of my dreams. I find it hard to accept interpretations given by Freud, Jung or modern-day shrinks. Although I am not equipped to read messages in dreams, I can draw some inferences from my experiences. One point I am quite certain, that is, there is no truth in ancient tales of kings, queens and princesses' dreams which foretold events to come. Such dreams were, and are, as unreliable as forecasts made by astrologers. The one strand that runs through dreams from infancy to old age is anxiety. They take different forms in one's life.
>
> In one's childhood they revolve around being deprived of the security provided by parents. Children often dream of the deaths of their parents. Such nightmares last till adolescence. During school and college years come fears of failure in exams; our dreams turn to finding ourselves in examination halls unable to answer any questions. It is about the same time we dream of finding ourselves in embarrassing situations like being unsuitably dressed in formal gatherings, or falling in space to wake up with a thud, or being able to fly. I have yet to fathom what they mean.
>
> With youth come erotic dreams. Oddly enough they are not about girls we love but often about those we find unlovable in waking hours. Erotic dreams persist throughout married life. The strange feature about them is that they do not involve spouses or women they have extramarital liaisons with, nor even find desirable, but usually those little known to them. I have also a lurking feeling that there is some connection between the kind of food we eat during the day and the pattern of dreams that follow. I have noticed,

1. Khushwant Singh "Dreams and Anxiety", *Hindustan Times*, New Delhi (March 15, 2003).

> when I am constipated my dreams are more vivid and in brighter colours. I have also noticed that as I get older and the day of final departure gets closer, the fear of death does not disturb my night's repose.

Dreams present us with bizarre arrangements of characters and situations, and often lack any logical sense of narrative. Time, place and even laws of gravity are defied. Animals speak to us, objects move, otherwise familiar and likeable characters behave monstrously; strangers pursue or help us; we visit unknown but fully realized landscapes.

Archetypal and Symbolic Dreams

A dream is not a thought. It is an image floating up from a subliminal state, complete in itself. As such, it is not subject to the strictures of conscious. It is pre-conscious and has no truck with time, place or demeanour. The images the dream presents have their own sufficiency and are specific to the message the dream is conveying. In this way the images appearing in the symbolic form are like a parable or metaphor to the dreamer.

Dr Jung called mythological symbols, zodiacal signs, and planetary signs as archetypal, and says they carry a meaning which is beyond the confines of personal life. We are all a subtle combination of all twelve signs of zodiac — emphasized in different ways by the planets and luminaries (Sun and Moon) and the way the signs were placed in relation to the earth's precise position in space at the moment and place of our birth.

An archetype is a symbolic motif that expresses itself in the same essential pattern. They have meaning to all humanity and appear across cultures and eras in the same form. The form of each archetype image will be specific to each individual, tribe or social group. Archetypes are inherited, primordial images that appear spontaneously from the depths of our unconscious. Archetype motifs appear frequently in art, and they are often expressed in individual dreams. Their peculiar power resides in the fact that they are unconscious manifestations of primtive instincts and aspirations. They can take many forms, and are often personalized in the artist's or dreamer's vision. Essentially, however, they are a primitive constellation of symbols that are intimately connected to the precognitive area of the psyche (the greater part of the psyche).

The archetype is one of the most powerful legacies of our unconscious heritage. Archetypes by nature are collective. They appear everywhere in human discourse, ancient and modern, whether that discourse is art, literature, tribal ritual or the dreams of an urban and thoroughly civilized individual of the late twentieth century. Archetypes are thus related closely to myth, which is the story-telling component of our collective history. We could characterize myths as the external ordering of the collective unconscious. And the collective unconscious is the domain of the archetype.

Young children can have vivid archetypal dreams. The key symbols of these dreams refer clearly to elements of which the child cannot possibly have had knowledge. These are not tales told in the playground, or even taken from fairy tales.

Archetypal dreams are a type of experience that may resist the standard analysis. These dreams are usually both more powerful and more ephemeral: powerful in the sense that they are especially striking; ephemeral in the sense that they hold meanings that transcend the nature of the everyday preoccupations with which you are concerned. These dreams tap into the broader rhythms of your life.

With symbolic images of dreams, the interpretation gets fudged. The sleeper producing a Freudian dream, in which a broomstick represents a phallus, has made an optical pun: he has connected a single visual form with two different functional contexts. The same technique is employed by the caricaturist who equates a nose with a cucumber, the discoverer who sees a molecule as a snake, and the poet who compares a lip to a coral. When Jean Cocteau underwent a drug-withdrawal cure, he drew human figures constructed out of the long, thin stalks of opium pipes. William Harvey, watching the exposed heart-valve at work in a living fish, suddenly visualized it as a pump — but the analogy between the gory mess he actually saw, and the neat metallic gadget, existed in his mind's eye only.

These, however, are rather dramatic examples of symbolic language for ideas, feelings and situations displayed in dreams. As a rule, visual imagery does not work in such a precise fashion. The visualizer rather feels his way around a problem and strokes it with his eye, as it were, trying to fit it into some convincing or elegant shape; he plays around with his vague forms like the couturier with his fabrics, draping and undraping them on the model.

Daydreams

The daydreaming results out of contemplation, most of the times. One drifts into the mode of contemplative thinking in an environment of intense light, usually dry and still air, and sometime a palatable music or sounds of cicada, cricket, or buzzing of bees. But still daydreams are not exactly dreams, although they belong to the same type of non-rational, non-directed thought. They are thought projections which often lead us to the new ways of seeing; they are lateral and creative, while also being unfocused and undemanding.

Daydreams reflect what the dreamer may or may not be in real-life. The subconscious, given a tranquil environment, projects to the daydreamer images of undeveloped potentialities or overlooked possibilities. Daydreaming is really about fantasy.

During daydreaming, unlike sleep dreaming, one remains in control and is conscious. Therefore, it is desirable to use daydreaming as a positive visualization exercise to achieve health, wealth and prosperity through right means.

When you have time during the day, drift to daydreaming, use imagination. Your miniature and mutinous mind is highly agile, thought undulations are highly vibrant — they cross alfa, beta and delta brain waves in quick successions or in a hotch-potch fashion; empty mind is a devil's workshop. Creativity could be at a very high or low ebb; or mind is in ESP (extra-sensory-perception) mode, you may have clairsentient, clairvoyant, clairaudient, or telepathic image; or even a fig of fantasy. The quick-silvery mobility of mind is always an asset for creativity.

Lucid Dreams

A lucid dream is one where the dreamer is aware that s/he is dreaming, in other words the dreamer's consciousness is awake but the dreamer does not wake up. The dreamer can, to a greater or lesser extent, control and direct the dream. Lucid dreaming can be learnt through proper practice, although it comes by itself at the proper level of human evolution.

A Dutch psychiatrist Frederic van Eeden[2] was the first to use the term "Lucid dreaming" in 1913. He wrote,

> In the lucid dreams the integration of the psychic functions is so complete that the sleeper remembers day-life and his/her own condition, reaches a state of perfect awareness, and is able to direct his/her attention, and to attempt different acts of free volition. Yet the sleep is undisturbed, deep and refreshing.

Frederik van Eeden's discovery is that:

(i) It is possible to become conscious while dreaming.

(ii) There is a dream-body. In lucid dreams there is the sensation of having a body — having eyes, hands, a mouth that speaks, and so on — which is perfectly distinct; while the physical body is sleeping and has quite a different position. In waking up the two sensations blend together, so to speak, and one remembers as clearly the action of dream-body as the restfulness of the physical body.

(iii) A lucid dream can be manipulated any way the dreamer wishes. The lucid dreams can also be controlled. There is,

2. Frederic van Eeden, "A Study of Dreams" *Proceedings of the Society for Physical Research*; vol. 26 (1913).

however, one caveat: you have to believe you can do it. There have been instances in which lucid dreamer's were unable to change their dream-scapes at will, but these seem to have been linked to lack of confidence.

(iv) Lucid dreams enable the dreamer to do many things that were simply impossible in the waking world, like flying or conversing with the dead.

(v) Lucid dreams tend to become visualization experiments. The familiar laws of physics are suspended, so that you can do anything you wish and go anywhere you want. You can achieve your ideal weight and height at the blink of an eye. You can fly to Sirus without a spaceship. You can meet anyone you wish, do anything you wish. You are limited only by the extent and creativity of your own imagination. And, since lucid dreams tend to be vivid dreams, the world you create can be so convincing that they are extremely difficult to tell apart from the world of your waking hours.

(vi) Lucid dreams can be utilized to induce insight into the future.

Since the dream-body influence goes far beyond the effect of waking-imagery to produce real physiological effects, scientists have now begun to speculate about the possibility of using lucid dreams to facilitate therapeutic processes. They may also help personal development, enhance self-confidence, and problem solving. They have already been successfully used as a tool to combat recurring nightmares. There are particularly interesting applications for the handicapped who can, for all intents and pursposes, regain full physical functionality during a lucid dream. Nor is this necessarily an empty illusion. One scientist has suggested that because of the body/mind interaction, sensorimotor practice of this type might help recovery from certain conditions, notably strokes.

The lifestyle benefits of lucid dreaming are also attracting considerable attention. The lucid dream has been compared to a flight-simulator which allows pilots to train without the possibility of a fatal crash. Individuals might "try out" various courses of action in a lucid dream to experience their consequences before putting them into place in the waking world.

Many lucid dreams — perhaps as many as 80 per cent of all reported cases — arise spontaneously when an ordinary dream turns lucid for no apparent reason. This is most likely to happen during nightmares or anxiety dreams, although there is evidence that any intense emotion, including embarrassment, anger, or joy, can trigger lucidity. Most people experience this type of lucid dream at least once in their lifetime but, exactly like an ordinary dream, may not remember it. Such lucid dreams tend to be short.

Some authorities suggest that the act of recording (on a small tape recorder) your dreams tend, in itself, to stimulate lucid dreaming. Whatever be the truth about this, it is a good idea to concentrate on simple dream reading, without worrying about lucidity, for two to three months before you start to apply lucidity techniques.

One of the world's leading authorities on lucid dreaming, Dr Stephen LaBerge of Stanford University developed mnemonic induction of lucid dreams (MILD) technique in 1990. This technique is applied after you have woken up from a dream and before you go back to sleep again. The first step is to remember the dream inasmuch detail as possible. Then, as you begin to drift back towards sleep sincerely intent that when you begin to dream again, you will realize you are dreaming. As in meditation practice, if your mind is drifting on to other things, gently bring it back again to your intention — I'm dreaming.

With your mind firmly focused on the intent of remembering, imagine yourself back in the dream from which you have just woken up. For this time imagine yourself realizing you are dreaming. Carry on with your visualization by imagining, in detail, how you would have changed the dream had you become lucid; then imagine yourself doing so in the lucid dream you are about to have when you fall asleep. Repeat your intent and visualization until you do so.

Another technique, wake-induced lucid dreaming (WILD) involves passing directly from the waking state into the dreaming state without losing consciousness. The best time to attempt WILD is immediately after waking in the morning or during the period of naps. Focus on your last dream and relax as you try to "reach" for it. Maintain concentration; if you allow your mind to drift, the chances are you will fall asleep. You are very likely to experience both visual and auditory hypnogogic imagery before passing into the dream state proper. After this you may well feel yourself sinking or floating out of your body, an experience similar to that of astral travel. Alternatively, you could find yourself "drawn" into the dream; one subject reported being grabbed by a wind. Even the most experienced practitioner may have a momentary loss of consciousness, but this should be extremely brief if it occurs at all. When the transition is completed, you will be dreaming and lucid.

To understand the importance of "lucid dreaming" we have to recall the classic works of Dr Freud of Vienna, the father of psychoanalysis. According to Freud's ideas the child is born with a well-developed unconscious but little conscious. However, as the child cannot speak and has no conscious memory, it has hitherto remained an inscrutable mystery what his unconscious was like; for when language, memory and the conscious are developed, the unconscious suffers eclipse, and is totally excluded from the child's waking thought.

During the flight of life, the conscious gradually obtains supremacy over the unconscious. In the adult brain, there is, as it were, still another level of mental activity — that of the foreconscious. The highest level or conscious consists of thoughts, feelings and desires uppermost in the mind at this moment; the next level, or foreconscious, consists of thoughts, feelings and wishes latent in the mind, and the lowest level is the unconscious, which consists of the repressed desires of early infancy. It is through his/her conscious that a person is aware of these remarks; it is his/her foreconscious that all the facts learned, feelings experienced and desires formed during his/her lifetime are stored; it is by his/her unconscious that his/her personality is fixed, and his/her satisfaction in life realized.

Lucid dreaming can heighten the awareness of the messages and images that the unconscious is formulating between inner (unconscious-sleep) and outer (conscious-waking) states and as desirable human goal, therefore lucid dreaming is a useful aid for integration-wholeness and health. One can confront fears and phobias through lucid dreaming exercises and get rid of the same, and also can enhance creativity of his/her own.

P.D. Ouspensky[3] the famous Russian mystic, practised lucid dreaming by deliberately holding on to his conscious awareness until he fell asleep. He found that by doing this, he could maintain consciousness even while asleep, and consequently watch and participate in his dreams.

When you go to bed physically exhausted, you are more likely to experience lucid dreams during night. Emotional problems can also create lucid dreams. However, you explore physical exhausion in preference to emotional stress.

Spirituality helps you to have lucid dreams at your command. Once you reach a certain stage in spiritual life, it becomes possible to change your dreams while they are taking place, and actually you create your own dream. But to do that, you must be able to maintain the dual consciousness of the dreamer and the dream, while you are dreaming, you know that you are dreaming — lucid dreaming. This was demonstrated by Swami Rama,[4] who even controlled his consciousness so as to produce beta, alfa, theta and delta brain waves, at his will, under strict laboratory conditions with the direction from Dr Elmer Green, at the Menninger Foundation in Kansas, USA, in 1977.

---

3. P.D. Ouspensky, *A New Model of the Universe*, London: Routledge and Kegan Paul Ltd., (1960).
4. Swami Satyananda Saraswati, *Yog Nidra*, Munger (Bihar): Yoga Publication Trust, 2003, p. 176.

The lucid dreams are directed "propulsions" and visualizations; through them one can achieve "self-realization."

On-demand Dreams

These dreams are sought to work as oracles (Oracle is the seat of some divinity, as of Apollo at Delphi, where prophesies were given out by the priests in answer to inquiries. "Search Seeing" is to be done in dreams. For example, if you wish to know your future lover, then you must sleep under a walnut tree to see him/her in your dreams.

To have dreams of your asking, the following techniques are used:

1. Yantra technique
2. Mantra technique
3. Tantra technique
4. Crystals technique
5. Programming technique

For on-demand dreams, keep your mind clear and as free as possible from rubbish material, and go to sleep without negative thoughts. A relaxed mind is most desirable for obtaining the dream on-demand. Follow a regular routine so far as bed and waking times are concerned. A routine you keep to without necessarily having to think about it, enables your body to slow down into a comfortable idling mode, and your mind to relax gradually before the sleep. Putting daisy roots under your pillow may help. Following a set routine so far as waking up is concerned can also be helpful. For instance, do not allow yourself to be shocked out of sleep by a loud alarm, but use either soft music or change in light levels to wake you gradually.

Avoid stimulating drinks such as caffeine, or alcohol. Caffeine stimulates the system making it more difficult to get to sleep initially, and again lowering the quality of the sleep itself. Whereas alcohol may relax one initially, it tends to cause wakefulness later during the night, disturbing and decreasing REM sleep.

Research in the brain activity has discovered that a signal of 18000 Hertz fed into the brain induces mystical feelings, which may result in hypnogogic and hypnopompic states suitable for desired dreams, with application of any of the techniques.

YANTRA TECHNIQUE

Those who desire to receive oracles through a dream, let them make an *yantra* or, say, a ring of the Sun pertaining to the oracle of well-being; the Moon regarding oracle of home life and mysteries of mind; Mars for redress from disputes, accidents and law suits; Mercury for travel, wealth and business; Jupiter for career and education; Venus for love life; and Saturn for fate and fortune. There are also images of dreams (available only in the Western World), which being put under the head when the person goes to sleep, give true dreams of whatever the mind had fore-determined.

MANTRA TECHNIQUE

There are many many *mantras*, which, if recited properly, will bring dreams of future events. However, only three of such *mantras* are given below to induce the desirable dreams.

Recite the following *mantra* during midnight in a complete naked posture. Then go to sleep. You will have answer to your problem in your dream.

om kirim do svaha

Recitation of the following *mantra* for 108 times will enable you to see through dreams all the auspicious events taking place in your life or which will come true:

om hreem laa hraa plakshmeem svaha

First recite the following *mantra* for 1008 times, thereafter recite 108 times at the time you are going to sleep. You will see auspicious and favourable dreams which will come true.

om shukle mahaashukle hreem shreem
ksheem avatara avatara svaha

TANTRA TECHNIQUE

Tantra for facilitating on-demand dreams is some "ash" which is kept under pillow during the night. The ash is prepared by burning a branch of a tree, after the branch is purified with *dhoop*. The branch should be of a tree in forest which is having Ambervel (a hard brownish-yellow or yellow resin). The branch is to be cut from the tree with Ambervel by the person seeking the dream. Think of a question for which you want the answer and sleep. You will receive the reply to your question in dreams during the night. In case the desired dream does not come up, repeat the process night after night till you are satisfied.

CRYSTALS TECHNIQUE

Hebrews believe that "Amethyst" crystal induces dreams and visions.

Jade is known as dreamstone, place it under your pillow for dreaming. Jade allows the release of emotions and provides solution in dream.

Tunnellite stimulates beta brain waves and can promote creativity through one's dreams.

Green Sapphire encourages the remembering of dreams.

Red Jasper allows dream recall, and is good for carrying the dream forward.

Diaspor gives clarity to dream recall, as though the person were watching a video.

Beta quartz is an aid in decoding dreams.

Lapis gives insights into one's own dreams. It makes possible a connection with the Higher-Self.

PROGRAMMING TECHNIQUE

If you wish to stimulate specific dreams for your own entertainment, progress or healing, you can learn to programme yourself to dream what you wish to dream. Programme yourself for success, wealth, health, romance, adventure, or any other type of need that you may have.

Simply say to yourself in a repetitious manner that "Tonight I will dream about . . . I will fully remember my dream when I wake up in the morning." Repeat this over and over just before you drift off to sleep and, with practice, you will begin to realize more frequent programmed dreams and be able to remember them better than you ever have had in the past. Because your mind responds, you will begin to have dreams of a very informative or revealing nature in total accord with what you have programmed into it.

The dreaming self is quite capricious, so to begin with you may not receive an answer on the night you request it. You may receive only a part of an answer, or nothing for several nights, and then a series of dreams which tell you what you need to know. It is a highly individual process, and no one can tell you how it should be. With time you will recognize your own pattern, but be prepared to be patient with yourself.

Prodromal Dreams

Dreams focusing on the physical body and its symptomology are characterized as "prodromal." Prodromic dreams normally warn us of health problems.

All along life, harmony and health are carted by our emotions, feelings and experiences. Should we bottle up the emotions and/or feelings, they are likely to explode as health hazard in our dreams or even along the journey of life, sooner than later.

Emotions can be as potent as bacteria. Depending upon your particular mixture of values and the state of satisfaction of your desires, you are set to emote in your own special ways. The quality and quantity of your own equilibrating devices determine the characteristics of your emotional responses. These reactions colour your whole physiology and psychology, determine the amount of civil war you will wage with yourself, and the quality of your dreams.

The outstanding emotion in a dream seems to have significance. S/he who is suffering from the feelings of inferiority, dreams that friends do not recognize her/him, that s/he falls down when trying to make a speech, or that he cannot get the tennis ball over the net. Overanxious individuals are subjected to defeat dreams repeatedly. They feel themselves rushing for aeroplanes which leave before they reach airport. Or, they open up their case of products to sell and find it empty. Love-hungry women dream of their husbands' "animalistic" sexual advances.

Your dreams of feelings emanate from your "world within" and are as individual as your fingerprints, with your "hidden me" retaining the key. Prodromic dreams can fashion a sort of psychic can-opener to unload the pent-up feelings which are spoil-sports to enjoyment, success, and health.

Invariably, nothing was found organically amiss with patients who have had bottled-up emotions and feelings. Fault-finding, nagging, and bickering are ways of thinking due to emotions; though they produce all the ills human is prone to get, they do not give rise to prodromic dreams.

Re-created Dreams

It was Fritz Perls who proposed the purpose of recreating your dreams. By doing so, you increase the potential of the dream, making it easier to analyse and extract optimum information.

The whole dream can be reconstructed like the original one, and the information can be extracted from it. Choose any person or object from your dream and ask for answers to your questions. This might evoke your Higher-Self intuitively to communicate with you. Or the person or object in the dream may talk to you or do something which may indirectly convey the information meant for you.

Re-created dreams are partially on-demand dreams.

Visitation Dreams

The dreams in which your relations, friends or foes — even those who are dead — appear, constitute visitation dreams. Their vivid appearence is due to your strong emotional bonds with them. In case of living persons, often these dreams have an element of telepathy. Twins, for example, often report dreaming accurately of events happening to their other counterpart, even if they are not in contact at the time. Close relatives or family members may dream of each other, particularly if a warning of some sort, or a cry for help, is implied in the dream. In this case, the sense of distress felt by the dreamer usually impels an action which validates the contents of the dream.

Dreams of people who are dead or near death may be equally distressing or demanding. There may be a feeling of guilt involved: perhaps the dreamer did not have time to say "good bye" to the dead loved one, or held repressed resentment which was never aired. In such cases, and if the dream is persistent and troubling, it is suggested that the dreamer confronts the problem, and expiates the guilt by, for example, writing a letter to the person in the recreated dream, or visiting the gravesite. In Hindu culture, people normally visit a temple or a holy place. In any case, as with all recurrent dreams, it is most important to address the uncomfortable emotions that are dredged up.

Repeated dreams of the dead are often reported in cases of the persons who had untimely death. In these dreams, the dead appears with an assurance, direction, warning or an urgent message. It may be that we are able to receive messages from beyond the other side, or events are being foreshadowed. It is better to heed to such vivid messages or warnings, because they are strong signals of either an internal or an external disharmony within the dreamer or around him/her.

Astral Travelling Dreams

We regularly astral travel (means leaving the physical body behind and moving around in the astral body) in our sleep — some people experience it more as a dream. But when you astral travel while you are asleep, you are extremely aware of everything that is going on. The colours are more intense and vivid and you feel more alive than you do during the day. These things do not happen in a dream.[5]

Shamans often travel to find glimpses of the future or answers to questions either through out-of-body experiences (astral travels) or dreams. If one goes into the details of such excursions, one would find many similarities in the two models of travel — astral travel and lucid dreams. Further, astral travel on-demand is parallel to dreams on-demand. Our usual dreams are involuntary astral travels.

Research is leading us to the conclusion that the REM images are dreams and the NREM images are astral travels. The main characteristics of astral travels are:

1. The subjects feel that they are leaving their bodies out of the top of their heads.
2. The subjects black out for a second at the exact instant their astral and the physical bodies separate.
3. The subjects' astral bodies float above the physical bodies for a while before moving away.
4. The astral bodies float again over the physical bodies before returning.
5. The subjects black out again momentarily as their astral body returns.
6. When the astral body returns too quickly, the subjects' bodies are buffeted and jolted.

The above observations are the study findings of Dr Robert Crookall.[6]

---

5. Richard Webster, *The ABC of Astral Travel, Transcending Space and Time*, New Delhi: New Age Books, 2003, p. 138.
6. Robert Crookal, *The Study and Practice of Astral Projection*, London: The Aquarian Press, 1961.

Sylvan Muldoon, an American Researcher,[7] believed that whenever you dreamed of flying, you were actually already astral travelling, even though your consciousness was still in your physical body. In the dream state, the astral body often moves right out of the physical body and floats ten or twelve inches above it. Thus, the dreams of flying or falling constitute conscious remnants of astral projections.

Implanted Dreams

Our dreams can be managed by others — the dreams can be conditioned and controlled from outside. When you are falling asleep, a certain programme can be given to you for the whole night, so that these will be your dreams for the night. And those dreams can be manipulated from the outside also. During the period you are falling asleep, there comes a moment, an interval, when you are not awake and you are not yet asleep either — just in between, that boundary line. That boundary line is the most sensitive part of your existence because you are changing the gears from one gear to another gear. Before you change gears you have to pass through the neutral gear, and when you are in a neutral gear anything can be put into your head. That's the whole secret of hypnosis : the neutral gear, the time when the previously programmed dream gets pushed in. That is the time when you are absolutely vulnerable; you cannot defend, you cannot argue.

Children are more vulnerable. The child can be told, "Go on looking at the roof continuously without blinking your eyes." A moment comes when the eyes become glassy; they are seeing and yet not seeing. That is the time when the neutral gear has come into existence. Wakefulness has gone, sleep has yet to come. It is the evening time; the day is no more, the night is entering. It is the most sensitive and suitable time gap. Say anything and it will go directly to the heart of the child. It will condition the child the deepest.

---

7. Sylvan Muldoon and Hereward Carrington, *The Phenomenon of Astral Projection*, London: Rider and Company Ltd., 1951.

You can condition, for example, a child (grown-ups are no exception) by telling him, "You will be dreaming of a great desert. For miles and miles there is nobody — sand and sand and sand, and you go on and on. . . ." And you can help the implantation of dream from the outside too. You have put the seed inside; then just a little heat near the feet, and the child will start dreaming of the desert, because the heat near the feet will give him the feeling of walking on hot sand. A little heat near the head and he will feel he is under the hot sun, and you have triggered. . . . You have done both the things: you have put the idea in the unconscious and you have triggered the process in the body. The child is bound to dream about the desert, and of course he will follow the programme that you have given.

This is the way people are brain-washed, and are made to work as remotely controlled slaves, soldiers, spys . . . the font of psychotronics.

6

Dream Healing

KABBALISTS believed that the dreams heralded illness, and should be used therapeutically by meditating on a problem before sleep and formally asking the dreaming mind to convey a healing message. The method, known to Jewish Kabbalists for centuries, is known today as dream incubation.

In classical Greece, dream incubation was a commonly employed method of healing. In temples called Asklepia, dedicated to the God of Healing, Asklepios, the supplicant patient underwent a long purifying ritual involving bathing, sacrifice and dreaming. Asklepios would appear in a dream, bringing a healing message. The dream was not interpreted; it was itself regarded as cure.

The practice of incubation by performing rituals and praying to the gods, in order to procure dreams in which cures of diseases are accorded, was formerly widespread in many cultures. The incubation would bring the dreamer into contact with the particular deity/saint and obtain a direct categorical answer to a direct specific question. Soliciting healing dreams subsequently grew into cults in many habitats and countries and was once very profitable to the priestly class and shamans.

The Indian parallel of shamans is *ojhas*. Shamans use dreams and ecstasy (through rituals) as tools of healing, whereas *ojhas* are conversent with ecstasy and Tantra techniques. As a rule, the shamans have taken recourse to dreams when they have difficult cases of healing. Shamans say they "send the soul" with a communication, in the dark or during the night.

Manchu shamans, and also Goldi shamans, go to sleep before the performance, and spirits are supposed to come into them during the sleep. The northern Tungus shamans also sleep, but ecstasy comes to them after half-conscious state is reached through ritualism (performance). Those half-conscious states are probably what the Western mediums experience as light trance. Some shamans may do healing in their dreams, during ecstasy, or in a normal state of concentration or desire in which they simply think strongly upon the object of their intent.

The Nineveh tablets, found in the tomb of an Assyrian king of the seventh century BCE, contain dream symbolic formulas for healing.

The Naskapi Indians of the Labrador Peninsula in Canada rely on dreams in their everyday life. Jung related that these tribes believe in an inner being called Mista-Peo, who directs the individual life in its solitary existence. The Naskapis often live alone, and listening to the promptings of Mista-Peo is regarded as essesntal for a whole life — a healthy existence.

Senoi people of Malaysia use dream oracles for health, wealth and happiness.

Dreams are referred to as "day residue." This means that most of our dreams are brought about by events or stimulation in our day-to-day lives that become symbolized by the subconscious in the form of dream images. Bodily needs, tensions and other emotionally charged feelings and memories are often released through dream imagery.

Among occasional drug or alcohol abusers, who maintain dream diary, one may find that dream mind brightens after indulgence in drug/alcohol abuse. The dreaming mind releases freely all the pent-up anxiety/tension on the subsequent night. This is not true for habitual abusers, in whom the brain activity healing process gets derailed and dreaming mind forgets "day residue" release function resulting in the fear psychosis or neurosis.

Tests have shown that many types of sleeping pills reduce rapid-eye-movement (REM) phase of sleep, which is the time when most dreaming and holistic healing occurs. All sleeping drugs tend to interfere with the natural sleeping patterns that are so critical to a person's psychological stability. Withdrawal from these drugs tends to increase REM sleep, which can lead to restless sleep and excessive dreaming, often including nightmares. Meditation can be helpful in alleviating these unpleasant effects as well as helping the patient to re-establish natural sleep pattern.

Freud has surmised that anxiety nightmares culminating in sudden, terrifying awakening are often prevalent in dreamers with diseases of the heart; while those with lung disease are prone to dreams of suffocation, crowding or fleeing. Such dreams warn us of the health problems.

If you wish to stimulate specific dreams for your own healing — learn on-demand dreaming or lucid dreaming. These techniques have been used to enable the patient to deal with his problems at the subconscious level, and to solve problems which were frustrating him/her. Americans have made lucid dreaming a therapeutic tool and a way of dealing with inappropriate feelings. Their technique is called "RISC," and has four stages which go something like this:

1. Recognize a negative dream as it occurs.
2. Identify the bad feelings.
3. Stop the dream.
4. Change the negative feeling into a positive feeling.

Many consultancy clinics have started giving training and guidance for RISC, as well as on lucid dreaming techniques of MILD and WILD.

In the field of psychiatry a dream may be interpolated in the psychic concatenation, which may be followed backwards from a pathetic idea into the patient's memory. The next step is to treat the dream itself as a symptom and solution of hysterical phobias, obsessional ideas, and the like. Wherever it has been possible to trace a pathetic idea back to those elements in the psychic life of the patient to which it owed its origin, automatically, the idea has crumbled away, and the patient has been relieved of it.

Potentially, each dream provides an opportunity to deal with some aspect of your accumulated *karma*. Since Tibetans believe dreams and waking consciousness are simply twin poles of the human mind, your reactions in dream are just as capable of discharging *karma*, or laying down fresh karmic traces, as your reactions in waking life. Unfortunately, most of us remain ignorant of the spiritual possibilities presented by dreams and incapable of taking advantage of them though they should not go unnoticed. For this reason, Tibetan dream yoga was developed. Among its aims is the centering of mind and "rlung" energy in the body's midline channel. It is one of the best yogas for healing.

Dreams, mind and consciousness are interlinked *vis-à-vis* health and harmony. Wills Harman of Stanford Research Institute, USA has explained the connection between mind and human consciousness and their role in the physical world. Harman proposed that mind is spatially extended (the extensive aspect); that mind is temporally extended (the protensive aspect); that mind is ultimately dominant over the physical (the psychodynamic aspect); and that conscious, subconscious and unconscious minds are joined (the concatenative aspect). Therefore, conscious mental activity can affact the things of the physical world — including the organs, tissues and cells that compose our body. Mind is an irrefutably genuine factor in the process by which health and disease unfold themselves. Hence, the oggly-gobbly delights of dreaming will result in healing.

Orientation by Dreams

Dreams are fixations of the past, fantasies of the present and foreshadows of the future. Our mind perceives them.

Ashok Bedi, a Clinical Professor in Psychiatry at the Medical College of Winconsin, USA, says in his book:[1] Dreams show us how the soul views our lives. As a general rule, a dream supplies the information that consciousness either does not have, or does not adequately perceive or value. By following very general rules of thumb will help you to orient yourself to your dream.

"Typically, dreams have recognizable dramatic structure: setting, development, turning point, and resolution. Sometimes, one or more of these elements is missing, in which case we have an unfinished dream." (Don't worry; from time to time, we all get dreams that are or seem incomplete. We can still work with what we have.)

"Dreams do not tell us what to do; rather, they provide a different view that may augment, modify, correct, complete or contradict our conscious position. As a rule, when a dream presents an extreme view of a situation, it is counterbalancing an equal, but opposite, conscious position. In other words, the truth lies somewhere in the middle.

"Working with your own dreams is challenging, because the dreams present the view that you do not consciously see. In other words, the dream fills in what your blind spot misses." (Often, it is expedient to work individually in a group with a therapist or analyst skilled in dream work.)

"Your dreams can tell you a lot more than what you know. Other people will often see meaning in your dream, where you see nothing but the images themselves. Take care that the people with whom you share your dreams are trustworthy and bear you no ill-will. In telling your dream, you are exposing the sides of yourself that even you don't see.

"Working on your own dreams is about the process of dream work, not its outcome. It's amazing. The "product" you end up with may not look like much, but the process you have engaged in works on you, and will subtly deepen your consciousness and inform it of

1. Ashok Bedi, *Path to the Soul : The Union of Eastern and Western Wisdom to Heal Your Body, Mind and Soul*, New Delhi: New Age Books, 2005, pp. 188-191.

the intentions of your soul. Here are the basic elements of dream work that you need to know. With practice you can acquire the fundamental skills.

"To catch your dreams:

1. Keep your dream notebook and pen or pencil next to your bed.
2. When you go to bed, suggest to yourself that you will recall a dream and write it down.
3. Write down your dream as soon as you wake up.
4. If you have had an interesting dream, try to trace it back from the point you remember.

"To work with your dreams :

1. Review the dream you want to work on. Revisualize the images; feel the emotions again; re-experience the dream. This brings it back to life.
2. Consider the structure of your dream. What is the setting? How does the action develop ? Is there a turning point ? What conclusion does the dream reach ? (Often, dreams end before the turning point or the conclusion, which implies that the development cannot go further at that point of time).
3. Contemplate each image. Note the feelings, memories, and impressions that arise when you experience each image, situation, or person in the dream. Stay with the image; circle around it; don't let your associations lead you far afield.
4. What does the dream appear to be commenting on in your life? Your relationships? How you get around in the world? The (emotional and mental) space you inhabit? What is opposing you or assisting you ?
5. Compare the current dream with other dreams where the same or similar people, places, themes, and images have

appeared. What changes do you notice? How is your presence in the dream now different than it was in the past?

6. After working on your dream, note how your emotional state has changed in the course of your dream work.

7. Honour your dream by carrying out some action or ritual in your working life that honours the images and intent of the dream."

For example, if a long-forgotten friend appears in your dream, first understand what aspect or quality of this friend that you need to activate in your life to deal with a persent situation. Additionally, pick up the phone and call your friend. If you honour your dream and its images by some sacred ritual, the dreams will honour and reward you by continuing to send helpful, guiding messages. This establishes a positive feedback loop.

Dr Bedi says: "In one of my recent dreams there was a huge, grey garbage truck that I was to drive to deliver food for my wife's catering business. I inquired of why we needed such a big truck, suggesting that a small, cute, yellow delivery van with her restaurant's logo on it would be more practical and functional. My friend and mentor, Dr Terrence Lear, was visiting us from England. Terry and I took this garbage truck for a ride. To my amazement, he said that he had a day's lesson in how to use this garbage truck as an amphibian vessel, so we sailed off to a small island on Lake Michigan with our families, and spent a day picnicking on the beach of this island. We had a small condo for the day that had a magnificent view of the Milwankee Skyline. I realized that this was no ordinary truck, and I just needed some brief instruction to explore its amphibian wonders.

"Consciously, I had been trying to simplify my life (like the elegant little yellow delivery van, but it always got complicated and burdensome like the large grey garbage truck. I decided to accept the cumbersome complexities of my life, including accepting my wife's restaurant business that obviously encumbered my conscious life. This, in turn deepened my soulfulness. I am honouring my *dharma* (Natural Law) by accepting that I must navigate this truck onto the waters of my unconscious and get a view of life from the outside, from island to mainland and relinquish my wish to be mainland and mainstream. Paradoxically, by accepting my *karma* of complexity, I have actually started to make my life simpler. To honour the dream, I went to the toy store and bought a cute yellow delivery van and a huge grey garbage truck. They now sit side by side in my study."

7

Dream Numerology

OCCULTISTS have observed, from time to time, that "numbers" appearing in dreams convey ideas, sensations and life-forces. A number may appear, say you are looking at a clock; or counting an object, or currency, or days or years; or as a number of lottery ticket; or as a number of house or street. According to experts, the dream-numerology assumes special significance and need to be validated by actions:

Zero (0) : It represents the path of celestial bodies in the universe — be it planets or electrons or photons. In dreams, anyone within a circle is safe from external attacks, for example, a child or an adult within the arms of the mother or a well-wisher. However, circles formed by a vortex are foreshadows of violence.

In dreams, a zero indicates a resting period. It also symbolizes a time for introspection, regeneration and sometimes death. In esoteric terms it stands for the unconscious spread over everything covering the entire cosmos; in practical terms the feminity.

One (1) : In dreams the number one is symbol of unification, initiation, and the highest status. It is vertical, erect and upright, thus a phallic symbol.

In dreams, it can appear in different forms, e.g. one standing monolith, one tower, one vertical pole, etc. When "1" appears in a dream, it is time to take a lead and display leadership.

Two (2) : It represents duality — positive and negative; good and bad; soft and hard; head and tail; bright and dark; beauty and beast; love and hate; masculine and feminine; anima and animus; real self (ego) and the imposed self (super ego); and so on — "Fight or Flight" syndrome. When "2" appears in a dream it is time for balancing tactics and strategy.

Three (3): The number "3" in dreams overviews the three phases of life viz. Generation–Operation–Destruction; past, present and future; memory, perception and fantasy; fan, friend and foe; fortune, fun and fate; right, left and front, etc.

In dreams it may appear as a triangle in some form or a structure with three sides, like a pyramid with three sides; or three roads reaching a spot or originating from a spot; even a three-barrel gun. When "3" appears in a dream it is for you to initiate a venture, execute the plan and achieve satisfaction. Practically it warns you to overcome lackadaisical behaviour. A dream may appear in the form of opening of the "third eye"— a vision.

Four (4): In dreams it may be symbolized by a square, rectangle or a cross. It represents: earth, water, air and fire; four co-ordinates of space-time continuum; matter, energy, emotions and thoughts; or four aspects of human nature: sensation, feeling, thought and intuition; etc.

As a cross it signifies the union of opposites, or one standing at cross-roads in situations of confusion or crisis. In case of dream of "4," the dreamer should carry out SWOT (strength, weakness, opportunity and threat) analysis and be practical.

Five (5): The number five is indicative of activity, will, romance, communication, and creativity in dreams — "Brain and Brown" prescription is to be followed with a dream of "5." The dream may contain components of all the five physical body senses — sight, smell, sound, touch and taste. To a sick person a dream may remind him/her of the five religious symbols in the esoteric fashion.

Six (6) : This number is reflective of love, diplomacy, generosity, changes, difficulties and struggles of a dreamer's life.

When "6" appears in a dream it is the time to set ideals of love and family life on the one hand and humanitarian services on the other. A dream may appear in the form of the activation of the sixth sense, "the mind".

Seven (7): The number symbolizes accomplishment, anxiety, illusion, unification, dynamism, loneliness and emotional cycle of the dreamer. It may be scanning of seven days of a week or the display of rainbow to represent "7" or direct dream of the number "7". It suggests you apply all the seven tones of sound and all the seven bands of light energy to make a mark.

Eight (8): It is forerunner for great activity, power and ambition. It forecasts huge money if the dreamer is willing to work for it. So when "8" or symbol of infinity "∝" appears in the dream it is time to use judgement and authority to enjoy power and position with material gains.

Nine (9) : It signifies the aggression of the dreamer. It also symbolizes perfection and spiritual attainment. It promises great fortune to the dreamer if s/he is hardworking.

Ten (10) : The number "10" is the combination of "One" of masculine trait with "Zero" of a feminine trait; resulting in a new beginning — birth; a soul in the new incarnation.

Eleven (11) : When "11" appears in a dream, one must withdraw from worldly affairs and achieve inner peace and spiritual awakening.

Thirteen (13) : Dreaming of this number may not presage good results; even hardwork may not pay dividends. Irritation is likely to occur.

Nineteen (19) : When you dream "19", "Fight or Flight" syndrome is bound to get triggered, and the end result is "flight."

Twenty-Two (22) : When "22" appears in a dream, it is a proverbial catch "22"enviroment. But if you complete your assignments with a sense of responsibility and dignity, you are on the way for name and fame.

Thirty-Three (33) : Appearance of "33" in a dream is an indication of spiritual perfection.

In general, remembering the numbers appearing in your dream forecasts good luck ahead possibly connected with the dreamed number or some root or derivative of it. If you had the rare experience of being aware of the number of people (or things) in your dream, it signifies an increase in personal power and/or prestige. To dream of numbers which you cannot recall on awakening predicts a period of confusion and surprises regarding the affairs of others.

8

Time Table

DREAMING, sleeping and slumber of the body are component stages of the state of rest of an organism — all living beings rest regularly.

As a baby, you dreamed about half of your sleep time. If you are between the age groups of ten to sixty, approximately a quarter of your sleep is spent dreaming. Beyond the age of sixty, there is slight increase in your dreaming time.

Dreams arise as energy patterns due to an awakening, release or explosion in the psychic body. They come of their own accord according to *yogis*, tantrics and occultists. These spiritualists have observed the relation between the timings of a dream and the period of fructification of the dream saplings, which is as follows:

1. First quarter of night sleep within one year;
2. Second quarter of night sleep within eight months;
3. Third quarter of night sleep within three months;
4. Fourth quarter of night sleep within two weeks;
   (i) Early morning within ten days.
   (ii) Just before sunrise within 100 hours.

However, the above schedule of eventuations does not conform to the cases of futurology. Any event which is foretold to take place, say three years or five years hence, related dream need not arise only in first phase of sleep, it can appear even in the last phase of sleep when we are about to awake, and the materialization be expected at the time forold in the dream. Prophetic and visionary dreams are the best examples. Of course, another exception to the above schedule being not applicable is in the case of the dreams of the past fixations.

Therefore, one can easily conclude that Hindu sages laid the main thrust on the dreams related to the foreshadows of near-future and having short-term implications.

The evolution of human being has been picturized by Max Heindel.[1] The evolution of your present life can be seen in your dreams as already outlined in the Introduction of this book, and you can take guidance and directive from dreams as they appear from time to time, says swami Atmananda.[2]

Further the Western outlook is that dreams of futurology or an oracular format or prophetic nature usually occur to you during the deepest part of your night's sleep; for most of you this will be between 2.00 am. to 7.00 am. By this time digestion has usually been completed, your body muscles are normally relaxed, and your mind is mainly free of the day's events and consequently of fantasies and fixations. Dreams which occur under these conditions are generally worth your efforts at interpretation.

So far we have discussed about the "time of the dreams." Now, we should differentiate between the "time of a dream" and the "time in a dream." The latter reveals whether the dream scene is related to the past, the present, or the future. However, it is very difficult to know whether we are dreaming of the present, past or future event, because our semi–unconscious mind does not differentiate between time spans, and hence does little to distinguish between past fixations — history, present happenings — thoughts and actions, and futurologies — fortune and fate; of course some exemptions are always there.

According to Einstein's "Space-Time continuum" theory, "time" is "Space"-related co-ordinate. Therefore, the time in a dream can be correlated and asserted by association with objects in the dream and

1. Max Heindel, *Occult Principles of Health and Healing*, New Delhi: Cosmo, Indigo Books, 2002.

2. Swami Atmananda *alias* Ravindra Kumar, *All You Wanted to Know About Dreams*, New Delhi: New Dawn, and Sterling Publishers (P) Ltd., 2002.

with the relative positioning of the objects in the dream scenario. For instance, objects that approach the dreamer denote the future and receding objects, the past; and vice versa for the dreamer moving away or approaching the object. And, a resting object denotes the present.

In dreams, space and time become interchangeable as in a black hole. The dreaming of something which is far away may indicate that it is far away in time. This may be future or past, depending upon the directive significance of the dream. A long way in front would be future, a long way behind would naturally be of the past. Near or close would mean recently, or, in the here and now.

9

Interpretations

THE dreams come from a part of brain that is primarily pre-linguistic; the older part which therefore tends to present its messages in picture rather than words, says David Fontains, a psychologist at University of Wales who specializes in dreams interpretation.

There are three techniques of dream interpretation. The first two have been covered by Raphael, an English astrologer of prominent standing. The three modes are:

1. Direct interpretation.
2. Indirect/Ciphers delineation.
3. Interpretation by association.

The third method goes back to Napolean's *Book of Fate,* which gives listing of associations. The associations used are of several kinds, but the direct association is common. In 1977, J. Allan Hobson and Robert McCarley of Harvard Medical School proposed the "activation-synthesis" hypothesis. They suggested that the dreaming consists of associations and memories elicited from the forebrain in response to random signals from the brain stem.

Interpretation is very important. There is no truth to the theory that every symbol in a dream has a specific meaning, as for example, a snake could be good omen for someone who worships snakes or it could also mean phallic symbol. But, research has certainly pinpointed a fact that dreams hold the keys to various problems affecting one's mental structuring. The right dream, interpreted correctly, could even change one's entire life. Therefore, it is important for all dreaming souls to watch and interpret the signals from their unconscious, which links us with ourselves, each other and the cosmos.

It would seem very much a specialist art to interpret dreams. This is simply because people can dream about thousands of differnt things. Acceptance of a peculiar language of dreams — pictographic, metaphorical, allusive — may give you the key. It is simply not sufficient to look for objectives, probabilities, or familiar behaviours. Nor is it sufficient to make facile equations. "The interpretation of dreams and symbols demands intelligence. . . . Even a man of high intellect can go badly astray for lack of intuition or feeling," said C.G. Jung.

A dream is full of images that are condensed. Freud once said that certain intensely charged thoughts will often compress themselves into one symbol, which by virtue of its intense and collective nature, may often be difficult to decipher at first glance.

For both Freud and Jung, interpreting a dream was like interpreting a difficult piece of text, which inevitably needed the input of the dreamer to attain any real enlightenment.

Some shilly-shally dreamers are always in a hurry to analyse their dreams. This can never be done unless there is a thorough understanding of the personality of the dreamer. That is why two different people may have a similar dream requiring an entirely different interpretation. Sometimes knowing a person's unfulfilled wishes or desires is enough, as the dreams are frequently dramatic wish fulfilments.

"Dream interpretation, however, should be presented in different forms to persons of different types of mind, whether a dream appears in the robust form and vivid colouring of a physical illustration or in the tenuity and paleness of a symbolic expression," said an unknown savant.

Dream interpretations fill volumes. Some psychiatrists and psychologists translate every detail, believing that each character, incident, or picture is manifestation (replica) for some underlying stress within their clients.

The interpretations from standard dream books sold in variety stores and over-the-counter, are only for the gullible, ignorant or superstitious mankind, as dreams never predict the future, opined by a few intellectuals. If you dream of dead, stop being superstitious. This does not mean that the dead are "thinking of you" or praying for you, since nothing can influence your dreams but your own thoughts, conscious or unconscious.

The Dream Work and the Task of Interpretation

Freud referred to the process by which latent dream is transformed into manifest dream as the "dream work." The reverse process, that of working back to the latent thoughts underlying the dream from the manifest content, is the task of interpretation. The method of free association is employed to recover the associative context which provides the material for analysis. Now, as we turn to Freud's ideas about the relations between the manifest content of a dream and the latent (unconscious) thoughts which are expressed in it, we begin to confront his broader conception of the nature of unconscious processes.

In the case of confused and apparently meaningless dreams, which are more common among adults, the dream work, in addition, produces distortion and hides of the latent wish. How is this accomplished ?

Freud identified a number of relations between the manifest content of the dream and the underlying (unconscious) thought which describe how distortion is accomplished. The five of the relations are briefly given below:

CONDENSATION

First the manifest dream is a kind of abbreviated translation of the latent thoughts. Some of the latent elements are omitted altogether. Others which have some common characteristics are blended together and expressed in the same manifest element of the dream. Still other latent thoughts suffer fragmentation; only a part, a suggestive illusion to the whole latent thought, is represented in the manifest dream.

Freud referred to this first relationship between manifest and latent dream elements, and the process underlying it, as condensation.

DISPLACEMENT

The second effect produced by the dreamwork is one of displacement. A latent element of the dream may be replaced, not only by a part of itself, but by something else which is remotely associated with it so that the manifest element is but a remote allusion to the underlying thought. In addition, the ascent in the dream may be displaced from the most important element to another which is less important. This shifting of emphasis is a further evidence of the operation of a censorship which would be best served if it were impossible to discover the thought alluded to in the manifest dream.

TRANSLATION

Third, the latent thoughts are translated into visual images. Objects and activities are given a concrete representation. Even abstract words and relations are usually represented in terms of visual images. Freud viewed this as evidence of regressive process. The earliest material of thought, he argued, consists of sense-impressions and memory pictures. Only later do words become associated with these images and get connected so as to form thoughts. In this regressive translation of thoughts into images, which retraces the development of thoughts from primitive sense impressions and memory images, all the more recent acquisitions of the thought process are stripped away.

SECONDARY ELABORATION

A fourth mechanism of the dream work Freud called secondary elaboration. The results of condensation, displacement, and translation of thoughts into visual images are combined into some kind of coherent whole which, in turn, further distorts the relationship between the manifest content and latent thoughts.

SYMBOLISM

Finally, in addition to these several processes which serve to distort the meaning of the manifest dream, there is a constant relationship between certain manifest and latent elements called symbolism. The symbols employed in dreams (usually of sexual organs, objects, and activities) represent what Freud believed to be the universal language of unconscious, a constant translation of latent thoughts into manifest elements which often make it possible to interpret a dream even without recourse to free association to discover the link between manifest and latent elements. The method of interpretation based on a knowledge of symbolism, was derived by Freud from folk tales, myths, jokes, and the poetical use of language as well as from his study of dreams, and the methods of free association were thus considered complementary techniques. Even after the work of free association is finished, certain dream elements remained meaningless unless they were interpreted as symbols.

The dream symbology incorporates the concept of archetype to explain why some dream images have a universal meaning applicable to all the human race, while other images are highly personalized and only concern an individual dreamer. God and devils of world mythology are instinctive/intuitive representations of archetype for the race and the tribe. The other archetype "the persona" is an individual person's conscious personality as opposed to his/her unconscious. It may give rise to dreams in which the dreamer appears naked or is ostracised in some way.

Yet another archetype "the shadow" is reflection of the weaker aspects of the psyche of an individual, and is epitomization of all the worst faults of the dreamer. The shadow appears frequently in bad dreams or nightmares. It can appear as a pursuer, a bringer of bad news, or any other threatening figure. In whatever form, the shadow is usually tied up with a feeling of fear.

The symbology method of dream interpretation might be described as the "blind method," since it treats the dream as a kind of secret code in which every sign is translated into another sign of known meaning, according to an established key. If the interpretation is undertaken by means of an allegorizing symbolism, there is no guarantee that the procedure will eventuate in success.

In the parlance of dream interpretation, the words "symbol" and "sign" are frequently used interchangeably. However an important distinction needs to be made between them. "Sign" designates something known, without hidden meaning. Typical examples are street signs that state the names of the street, or signs on buildings identifying the occupants or businesses or signs of the changes of season (such as the reappearance of robbins in springs, or the migration of geese, or the sprouting of crocuses).

A "symbol," however, means more than what it literally is; a symbol is the best possible expression for things not fully known. Signs may inform us, amuse us, or arouse our curiousity; yet they are not mysterious. When something stirs emotions in us that we cannot fully explain, we are responding to a symbol. One person's symbol may be only a sign for another person. Collective images, like the flags, or the Christian's cross, may be symbols for some people, but only signs for others. It all depends on the way the image affects us, and whether or not we can fully explain the meaning in the image.

Symbols are images, events, people, or things that for us, are pregnant with meaning. Whenever we are fascinated by something whose meaning we cannot exhaust, try as we may, we are dealing with a symbol. Unfortunately, the term "symbol" is often used very imprecisely to designate any image. A company's logo for example, is an image, a sign, but not a symbol, since its meaning is explicit and centric. The red plus meaning "doctoring" is likewise a sign. The essence of the symbol is that we can't say enough about it; if only we could find the words, we would say more. Its meaning seems limitless. It is the best possible expression for something we don't fully know or understand.

Symbols appear when consciousness and unconsciousness are at odds. Health and wholeness are contingent upon the degree of relatedness and co-operation between our conscious minds and all those activities outside of our waking awareness that we call "the unconscious." Dream symbols free from subjective or objective prejudices can be appraised by consciousness in man as in two mirrors facing each other. Both can be images or reflections of the other.

Analysis

Finally, in the analysis of dreams, Freud found that he could not avoid the assumption, "that there are processes and tendencies in mental life, of which we know nothing; have known nothing; have, for a very long time, perhaps even never, known anything about that at all."

A pioneer psychoanalysist, and contemporary of Freud and Jung, Sandor Ferenczi has said: "As a rule, a dream is not to be translated into other languages because every tongue has its own dream-language."

A dreamwork, however, does allow the dreamer to decipher the interrelationship between multiple images, and gives fresh insight into their own psyche. And the idea that the dream concerns itself chiefly with the future, whose form it surmises in advance — a relic of the prophetic significance with which dreams were once invested — now becomes the motive for interpretations.

Dreams contain much hidden contents, invariably, which simply cannot be interpreted literally. Those who believe their inner night theatre to be exposing the "world within" or predicting the future are being very pseudo. Serious dream interpretation should be left to the experts! In the area of psychiatry, dream analysis and interpretation has advanced to the status of a scientific study.

Since it is impossible to find a man twice in exactly the same mental state (*yogins* and meditating monks, awakened people and enlightened persons are exceptions — their minds are always in ecstatic state), it is equally impossible for him to dream the same dream twice (precise repetition) which suggests that dream interpretation can be made only approximately.

Exemplifying Dreams

It has already been suggested that the meaning of your dreams presents a more difficult phase to explain. But you will get nowhere, however, if you indulge yourself in the frauds that popular dream books bring you (and this book is no exception) — beware. There is no dream book written or sold in the world that can intelligently or honestly explain the meaning of anyone's dreams. It is usually a very complicated task. While there is no simple formula for discovering the complete meaning of a dream, there are some clues as to how to go about it as in the following examples:

EXAMPLE ONE

An army officer had a recurring dream in which all his men were dead. Staring at the bodies of his dead men, he would hear marching feet of the army approaching. He would start to shoot at them, and as they approached, he found that they were not the enemy at all, but the mothers and fathers of his men. Although he would keep shooting through them, the marching parents would keep coming at him.

Now let us analyse this dream. To do so, however, requires a thorough understanding of the personality of the dreamer — the army officer. He was a young, idealistic person who had developed real Comeradeship with his men. He felt very keenly the responsibility of leading his men into battle. When anyone of them were hit, he would have feelings of guilt, feeling that he personally had let them down. While he dreaded informing the parents, he would in each case, personally write a gentle letter. Through it all, he continued to imagine that it was due to his personal shortcomings that many of his men were killed.

This dream should now begin to take on a fairly obvious meaning. The parents come to haunt him, while staring and pointing at him accusingly. But is this dream any different from his waking thoughts? His deep-seated feelings of guilt are also present when he is awake, but his dreams which are but a continuation of his daily thoughts express them much more dramatically.

This should give you the first major clue to the meaning of your dreams, namely that they are but a dramatic continuation of your daily thoughts. For just as there is continuity between waking and sleeping which concerns our bodies, there is also a continuity that concerns our minds.

EXAMPLE TWO

A dream that a woman relates: She is a stenographer and receives a letter which is addressed to her young and attractive employer. In order to tease him she will not let him have it. He then comes into her office and attempts to snatch the envelope while she runs with it around the office desk.

How would psychoanalysists interpret this stenographer's dream? The desire of the stenographer to be made love to and be seduced by her young and attractive employer is symbolized by the envelope and the chase. The envelope represents the female genitals, or in this case, her virginity. She wishes to surrender the envelope to him, but does not do so without first coyly evading him by running around the room.

"Well, how did the dream end?" Then you ask her. "Oh, I gave him the envelope and he tore it open," she freely answers. All that is missing for a perfect Freudean dream is to have him open it with a letter-opener from his desk!

Freud proposed the idea of symbolization in dreams, in which a symbol such as an envelope or letter-opener represents an idea. Thus anything long or pointed, such as sword, whip, tree, snake or letter-opener, would be symbolic of the male sex organ, while rooms, receptacles, bags and such, would be symbolic of the female organs. Dreaming of mice or running up or down a stairway would be symbolic of the sex act itself — since mice ordinarily run in and out of little holes. This ordinary moral stenographer could not consciously allow herself to entertain the disturbing wish of being seduced by her attractive employer. In sleep, however, her wishes insist on gratification, although the eagle-eye "dream censor" is careful to disguise her wishes in the garb of a more socially acceptable type.

One's dream symbols and manifest-contents must of course be interpreted in relation to the dreamer's personality and complexes, since dreams are not only fundamentally wish-fulfilling, but express, in distorted form, the anxieties and frustrations of the individual.

EXAMPLE THREE

One day an old lady in her early seventies came into a psychiatrist's office for consultation. She expounded all her ailments, real and imaginary, but seemed most concerned about a recurring dream in which she was diligently pursued by a personable young man whose intentions seemed dishonourable. The doctor was properly sympathetic and advised her how she might sleep more soundly. In a few days she returned, still woeful. "Don't tell me you are not sleeping better nowadays," teased the doctor.

"Oh, I'm sleeping just fine," the patient replied, "but to tell the truth, Doctor, I certainly miss that young man!"

The dream needs no interpretation — does it?

EXAMPLE FOUR

Here is an illustration of how physical stimuli are turned into your dream content. You may have dreamt that you are looking for a place to urinate. Pressure on a full bladder sending stimuli to the brain would ordinarily force you to awaken and to relieve the tension of this urge, but the dream, protecting you from disturbed sleep, keeps leading you to places where you may satisfy your urge. To prevent embarassment, however, you may find that there is always someone in your dream who pops in, to watch you or spy upon you, thus preventing your normal expression.

In many ways, your dreams protect you from waking up and disturbing your rest. Thus, if you are thirsty, you will dream of water; if you are hungry, you will dream of food; and if you are starved for romance — well . . . you will just dream.

EXAMPLE FIVE

Barbara Garwell's life as far as she can remember was full of premonitions in her dreams. She has had dreams about many of the world's major events before they actually happened. One of such dreams is as following:

In September 1981, Barbara dreamt of a warm country. There was sand in the place. She saw herself in a stadium where there were military men with coffee-coloured faces. They were wearing olive-green uniforms. In front of these men was a row of dignitaries in dark suits. Suddenly, the men in olive uniforms ran forward and pumped bullets into the chief of the dignitaries.

A page of her "Dream Diary" could have been like:

Dream number : 33
Date : 11-09-1981
Time of dream : 3.30 a.m.
Time in dream : Forward (Future)
Atmosphere : Warm
Theme : Assassination
Movement : Run
Objects/Signs : Stadium, soldiers, etc.
Colour : Olive-green
Previous association : Nil
Mood : Tense.

Three weeks later, on 6 October 1981, President Sadat of Egypt was assassinated by members of his bodyguards as he reviewed his troops at a ceremony. The assassins were with coffee-coloured faces, wearing olive-green uniforms exactly the same as Barbara had dreamt.

EXAMPLE SIX

Miss Bloom narrated her recurring dream. "I have been dreaming a lot recently about two brown dogs who seem to get along well but suddenly start to fight. There is nothing I can do to stop them. After this dream, I always wake up with a jolt."

Here the key words are : Two, dogs, fight.

Dreams that involve two people or animals fighting are often about the dreamer and someone towards whom s/he feels antagonistic, even though the dreamer does not actually star in the dream. Only the dreamer would be able to identify the object of this secret resentment or jealousy with any accuracy.

EXAMPLE SEVEN

Here is a dream of a young girl with numerical content and possible explanation.

> I had a very strange dream as a teenager, since when it has occurred a few times. I would dream I was getting dressed in the morning and when I want to put on my brassiere, there were three cups instead of two; I remember feeling terrified.

Here number "three" is in focus. The dream clearly reflects doubts about sexuality and doubts about developing in a normal way during adolescence — the three matrices of the life, viz. male, female and growth.

EXAMPLE EIGHT

A young boy relates his father's dream: One early morning, Krishna, a distant relative of ours dropped in. She is a very fat lady. She lives in the same locality as we. Her house number is 7/22 while ours is 22/7. Krishna said that she had a message for my father, who was still asleep. So she just chatted with my mother while waiting for my father to wake up. Some moments later my father woke up. "I've seen a very good dream," he said with a smile. "Tell us what you saw," said Krishna. "In my dream," said father, "I saw myself waiting outside a hospital room and a very fat nurse came and told me that Naresh (my eldest brother) has been blessed with a son."

Krishna broke into a smile and undoing the folds of her *dupatta* brought out a postcard. Passing the postcard to my father she said, "I'm that very fat nurse and here is the good news."

It was a letter from my brother's father-in-law carrying the news of the child's birth. It had reached Krishna's house because the address on it was wrongly written as 7/22 instead of 22/7.

EXAMPLE NINE

A young manager relates his dream: I leave my home right on time, and inching my way through extra long miles of slow and noisy traffic, laden with frayed nerves and road rage, reach my office. Late for work, I open my office door and find the boss pacing up and down inside the room. I stand stunned and humbled. The boss looks at me with a glint in his eyes and gives me a nice dressing down. I look at the paperweight on the desk and long to hit a bull's eye but, instead, fear dawns on me and am awake before mumbling an apology.

This dream is a xerox copy of the everyday anxieties and adverse work environment. The dream is a replay of the dreamer's repressed emotions of frustration and anger due to his uncompromising boss, who washes him up with profound sweating every now and then, and his inability to even pick up a file and hurl at the boss.

Interpretations of dreams are different from place to place, and often from generation to generation, although judging by the book stalls there are plenty of people who think they understand what it all means and can offer a simple list of explanations.

Dream Directory

You can have a most amusing and perhaps instructive time considering the meaning of your own dreams. To do so, however, you must think of them immediately upon awaking or they will be forgotten. By association, fragments of a dream may be recalled. Ask yourself, "What do the things I dreamed about represent to me?" "What unconscious thoughts might this dream be expressing?" Make sure the dream is potentially oracular or futuristic or prophetic one and not merely of the "garden" variety. Then by association or bisociation build-up a theme from the meaning of key words.

Look at any book on dreams (and this one is no exception), it is like a dictionary with pages of dream themes each with a short explanation.

In order to make the task of finding meaning of your dream easy, the direct interpretations for key words of any dream are given in alphabetical order (without short explanation, a deviation from other books). If there are more keywords in your dream, collect the interpretation for all of these and then synthesize them suiting your circumstances and environs.

Abandon - *A person* – Loss of friends and favours.
- *You are abandoned* – Troubles are approaching.

Abbey - Comforts and peace of mind.

Abdomen - *To see* – Pleasure with trauma.
- *Swollen* – Difficulties will be overcome.
- *Blood oozing from* – Foretells tragedy in family.

Abhor - Triumph over your foes.

Abnormal - *Man with wings* – You will cruise to heights and fame.
- *Man with horns* – You will torpedo enemy successfully.
- *Man with tail* – You will cross all hurdles.
- *Amphibian* – Swim to success.

Aboard - *A ship/an aeroplane* – success.

Abode - *You are in* – Sudden changes in fortune.
- *Ejected out of* – Difficulties.

Abortion - Good news.

Above - *Anything hanging above* – Worldly prospects will improve.
- *Anything falling from above* – Bad omen.

Abroad - Change of lifestyle.

Abscess - Good fortune after sickness.

Abscond - *Yourself* – Danger of acting dishonourably.
- *Another person* – Disloyal friends.

Absence - *You grieve* – you will get a long-lasting friend.
- *You rejoice* – You will get rid of an enemy.

Abundance - Desire for independence.

Abuse - Quarrels and losses.

Academy - Loss of position.

Accept - *Job* – Good omen.
- *Invitation* – Depression.
- *Gift* – Social activity.
- *Bribe* – Disrespect, troubles.
- *Alms* – Worries.

Accident - *To see* – Obstacles in plans.
- *By knife* – Be careful, may snap association.
- *While travelling* – Impending illness.

Accordion - *Hearing it* – Disappointment.
- *Playing it* – Conjugal happiness.
- *Out of tune* – An unhappy state of mind.

Accounts - Loss of trade due to bankruptcy of clients.

Accusations - *Accuser* – Quarrels with associates.
- *Accused* – Minor embarrassment.

Ache - Temporary discomfort.

Acorns - Speedy results, wealth and prosperity.

Acquaintance - Continued friendship.

Acquitted - Victory over enemies.

Acrobat - *To see* – Beware of rivals in the matter related to affairs of the heart.
- *A woman* – Hinderences in business.
- *Performing* – A dangerous scheme for you.
- *Falling* – Scheme should not be undertaken.

Actor - Freedom from want and worry, avoid speculation, fame.

Actress - Love affair, auspicious events.

Addition - Confusion in adding numbers means worries.

Adieu - Ill-health and sorrow.

Admiral - Desire for power.

Admired - Sincere friends.

Admonish - Good understanding between partners.

Adopted - Bereavement in the family.

Adornment - *For woman* – Lack of means to have decent living.
- *For man* – Poverty.

Adultery - *Commit it* – Reflects guilt complex and anguish.
- *Resist it* – Prosperity.

Advancement - Success.

Adversary - Will overcome impediments.

Adversity - Prosperity.

Advice - *Give* – Respect, success.
- *Take* – Added obstacles.

Advocate - Prominent placement for benevolent purpose.

Aeroplane - *To see* – Improvement in matters of heart, gain.
- *Taking off* – Hopes for future.
- *Sitting in* – Desire to attain success, apprehension.
- *In flight* - Fulfilment of desire.
- *Crash* – Failure of plans.

Affection - Honourable intensions.

Affiliation - Dreadful enemies, severe illness.

Affliction - Change of residence, early marriage.

Affluence - Poverty.

Affront - Annoyance and discontent.

Afraid - Valiance.

Age - Sickness and premature death.

Agony - Prosperity and good health.

Air - *Clear* – Success.

- *Clear and fine blue* — Good omen.
- *Thick and dark* – Disappointments.
- *Streaked with white* – Difficulties.
- *Streaked with red* – Sickness.
- *Calm* – Happiness.
- *Cold* – Unhappiness.
- *Hot* - Punishment.
- *Humid* – Possibility of being deceived.
- *Foggy* – Advised to change your plan of action.
- *Stormy* – Illness and/or being in danger.

Album - Search for new admirer, small success.

Ale House - *In it* – Means enemies.
- *Drinking ale* – Deception by flatterer.

Alien - Abiding friendship and love.

Alley - Sexual desire. Hard pressed for time.

Alligator - Rivalry in affairs of heart, opponents.

Almonds - Beware of troubles ahead, profitable journey.

Alms - *Refuse to give* – Misery.
- *Freely given* – Joy and long life.

Altar - Unsatisfactory results. Marriage vows.

Aluminium - *Pots and pans* – Happiness in domestic affairs.

Ambulance - Expect sickness and poor health.

Amethyst - *To receive* – Good luck.
- *To lose* – Trouble in love affairs.

Amputated Limb - Grief of friend or close relative.

Anchor - Stability in everyday life.

Anecdotes - Esteem in high quarters.

Angel - Legacy to come, good news, better prospects.

Anger - *Being angry* – Awful time awaits you.
- *A friend angry* – Will gain favour.

Angling - *Catch fish* – Prosperity.

- *No catch* – Frustration.

Angry - Making and having good friends.

Animals - *To see* – Business success, new business. Lust for sex.
- *Domestic* – Civilized outlook.
- *Wild* – Untamed tendencies.
- *Monstrous* – Expression of fear.

Annoy - Enemies around you.

Ants - *To see* – Business improvement, speedy marriage.
- *Killing* – Business liquidation.

Anvil - Success and long life.

Anxiety - Troubles will pass away.

Ape - *To see* – False friends.
- *Clinging to a tree* – Troubles from a false friend.

Apparel - *Have good clothes* – Want and penury/gains.
- *Have no clothes* – Prosperity.
- *Have white* – Favours from public.
- *Have black* – Bereavement of a dear one.
- *Have blue or purple* – Aprobation of friends.
- *Have scarlet* – Uneasiness by misconduct of children.
- *Have grimson* – Long life and moderate fortune.
- *Multiple colours* – Myriad fortune.
- *New clothes* – Success in undertakings.

Apples - *To see* - Unexpected good news, happiness in married life.
- *To eat* – Not so happy prospects.
- *Ripe and on tree* – Will realize your hopes.
- *On ground* – False friends.
- *Spoiled* – Typify hopeless efforts.

Applause - *Gaining* – Defamation of character.
- *Giving* – Solution to difficult situation.

Apricots - Poor health, success in love, speedy marriage.

Apron - *Good condition* – Favourable omen.
- *Torn* – Family feuds. Slander.

Arch - *To see* – Appreciation of your merits.
- *Walking under* – Disappointments.

Arm - *To see* – Good health.
- *Hairy arm* – Impending imprisonment.
- *Using right arm* – Fortune.
- *Strong arm* – Unexpected success.
- *Weak arm* – Fortunes are about to suffer.
- *Broken arm* – Ill luck.
- *Right arm cut-off* – Death of near relative (male).
- *Left arm cut-off* – Death of near relative (female).

Armchair - Peace at home and a happy long life.

Army - Bussiness success.

Arrested - Worries.

Arrow - *Hitting target* – Sure success.
- *Missing target* – Failure.
- *Hitting you* – Enemies.

Artist - Beware of making changes.

Ascend - *To top* – Will overcome difficulties.

Ashes - Beware of rashness, careful thoughts.

Asp - Sexual urge, an enemy, an obsession.

Ass - Patience and humility will help you to overcome misfortune.

Assassin - Shun all pretending friends. Lend no money.

Asylum - *You are in* – Coming personal affliction.
- *Inspecting* – Will help distressed.

Atonement - Admiration from seniors.

Attorney - Advice would be helpful to solve problems.

Auction - *Buying* – Gain, business expansion.
- *Watching* – Business success.
- *Awakens you* – be watchful in business.

Aunt - Misunderstanding and criticism.

Automobile - *To see* – News to arrive.

- *Drive* – Financial gains.
- *Desire for* – Desire for financial gain.
- *Ride* – warning of poverty.
- *Miss ride* - Troubles averted.
- *Wrecked* – Warning of rivals.
- *Own a car* – Gift to arrive.
- *Drive a car* – Freedom.
- *Drive alone* – New surroundings.
- *Drive with wife* – Long life.
- *Drive with children* – Happiness.
- *Travel in a car* – Strive for freedom.
- *Travel with woman* – Scandal.
- *Meeting with an accident* – Monetary gains.

Axe
- *To see* — Happiness after struggle (American).
- *Sharp* — Advancement.
- *Blunt* — Slowing in business.
- Rethinking and replanning required (English).

Baby
- *To bear* – Urge for sexual pleasure.
- *To have* – Danger of temptation.
- *Happy* – Success in heart affairs.
- *Smart* – Good friends.
- *Beautiful* – Happiness.
- *Taking first step* – Difficulties in business.
- *Walking* – Independence.
- *Nursing* – Omen of deception by known people.
- *Sleeping* – Desire for mate.
- *Crying* – Failure of love affairs, trials and trauma.
- *Sick* – Death in family.
- *Helpless* – Disappointment in love.
- *Many babies* – Abundance in life.

Bachelor
- *Young* – Happiness. Meeting with lover or a friend.
- *Old* – Likely to die.

Back
- *To see yours* – Uneasiness of mind.
- *Broken* – Scoff by enemies.

- *Bone* – Health, success in love and business.

Backbite - Praise from higher ups.

Bacon - *Eating* – Sorrow.
- *Buying* – Death of a friend.

Badger - Prosperity through industry.

Baffled - Success.

Bag - Something surprising to happen.

Baggage - Success, be aggressive.

Bagpipes - Poverty.

Bail - Trouble by unscrupulous person.

Bailiff - Favourable change.

Baker - Successful conclusion of a problem.

Baking - Ill-health in the home, sorrow.

Balcony - Difficulties, sickness, business rivalry.

Bald - Disappointment.

Ball - *Sports* – Business promotion and social aclaim.
- *Dancing* – Signifies ambition and wealth.

Ballet - Infidelity, jealousy, quarrels.

Balloon - Expect a surprise, difficult assignments.

Banana - *To see* – Beware of your lover.
- *To eat* – Foretells a tiresome venture.
- *To trade* – Non-productive interest will accumulate.
- *Decaying* – Disagreeable enterprises.

Bandit - Desire for sex or union.

Banishment - Peace and honour.

Bank - *Deposit money* – Money to come.
- *Withdrawal* – Financial difficulties and/or loss.
- *You are clerk* – Loss of job and money.

Banker - Profits to increase.

Bankrupt - Avoid discreditable tasks.

Banner - Visit to foreign Country.

Banquet - *To see* – Prosperous times.
- *Dining at* – Good luck.

Bar - Feeling of insecurity.

Barber - Good prospects in your job. Disease worries.

Barefoot - Fortune in speculation.

Barley fields - Your sickness or death of a relative.

Barn - *Filled* – Health, wealth and long life.
- *Empty* – bad times.

Bartender - Seeking good fortune.

Baseball - Desire for harmony and team work.

Basin - Good luck through friends.

Basket - *Full* – You will overcome obstacles.
- *Empty* – Beware of your habits. Failure.

Basketball - Expect a fair deal from others.

Bath - Mental contentment. Business expansion.

Bathing - *In sea* – Business expansion.
- *In river* – Mental contentment.
- *In hammam* – Removal of worries.
- *In pond* – Gain of respect.
- *With cold water* – Happiness.
- *With hot water* – Grief and sickness.
- *With clear water* – Prosperity and success.
- *With muddy water* – Poverty, poor health.

Bathroom - Disease, worries.

Bats - Unpleasant experience.

Battle - Success, good health, dissension.

Battlefield - Quarrels.

Bayonet - *To see* – Fear of someone close.
- *In possession* – Be alert to events.

Badger - Gain of wealth.

Beach - Need for relaxation.

Beaconlight - Troubles will fade away.

Beads - *To see* – Hard work ahead.
- *Good one* – Good luck.
- *Wearing of* – Warning of discord.

Beans - *To see growing* – Contension.
- *Eating* – Sickness.

Bear - *To see* – Rivalry in love affair. Loss through carelessness.
- *To kill* – Overcome trouble.

Beard - *Your own full beard* – Good fortune.
- *Woman dreaming of* – Loss of husband.
- *Cutting it off* – some loss.
- *To Shave* – Removal of worries.

Beat - *Children* – Dutiful and loving children.
- *Others* – Unrestful mind.

Beaten - *Yourself being* – Unhappiness.
- *Others being* – Loss of money.
- *Cat being* – Treachery.
- *Dog being* – Fidelity.
- *Horse being* – Happiness.
- *Snake being* – Victory.

Beating - *Someone* – Grudge is to be settled.
- *A friend* – Contentment.
- *Own children* – Happy events to follow.
- *Spouse* – Happiness for both.
- *Mistress* – End of love affair.
- *Husband* – True relation.
- *Wife* – Strengthening of relations.
- *An animal* – Damages in one's own affair.

Beauty - Sickness and debilitated strength.

Bed - *To see* – Freedom from worries.
- *Being in* – Early marriage.
- *Making it* – Friends will be added. Change of

residence.
- *Sleeping in other's bed* – New opportunities.
- *Sick people in bed* – Unhappiness.

Bed room - Journey, happy events.

Bee - *To see* – Hardwork required for success and honour.
- *To be stung* – Financial loss.
- *Buzzing* – Increase in business.

Beef - *To see* – Will depend upon others' bounty.
- *Eating* – Live in plenty.

Beer - *Drink good* – Success in love and business.
- *Drink bad* – Expect troubles.

Beetles - *Creeping down* – Slander.
- *Killing* – Will overcome slander.

Beets - *Eating* – Troubles will flee away.

Beggar - *To see* – Loss of valuables, seeking help of friends.
- *To see old* – Loss of property.
- *Help him/her* – Disillusionment.
- *Refuse alms* – Your resources need checking.

Beheaded - Separation from loved ones, reversals.

Bellows - *Blowing the fire* – Trouble.

Bells - A difficult problem is to be solved.

Beloved - Faithfulness.

Bench - Expect a change.

Bequest - Troubles and losses.

Bereavement - Wealthy marriage, prosperous partnership.

Berries - *Black* – Illness.
- *To eat black* – Loss of money.
- *Raspberries* – Embarassment.
- *Strawberries* – Long-awaited pleasure.
- *Eating above two* – Love and affection will be reciprocated.

Bet - Risk to personal safety and avoidable troubles.

Betel leaves - *To see* – Fortune.
- *To eat* – Enmity with friends.
- *To receive* – Sexual intercourse.

Betting - *On races* – Losses in business.
- *On table* – Take care before investing.

Bicycle - *Uphill* – Bright outlook for the future.
- *Downhill* – Warning of misfortune.

Bigamist - Uncontrollable emotions. Suspicion of relatives.

Billiards - *Players around* – Troubles.
- *No player* – Unknown enemies.

Birds - *To see* – spiritual outlook to develop.
- *On tree* – Unexpected happiness.
- *In cage* – Good news.
- *Flying* – Prosperity.
- *Singing* – Happiness.
- *Talking* – Warning about gossip.
- *Feed* – Receive honour.
- *Wounded* – Sadness due to a member of family.
- *Catch* – Prosperity and gain.
- *Behead* – Visit different places.
- *Kill* – Difficulties ahead.

Bird's nest - *Eggs in* – Will have property.
- *Baby in* – Excellent business arrangement.
- *Empty* – Gloom.

Birth - *For married woman* – Normal delivery, legacy foretold.
- *For unmarried women* – Loss of virtue/lover.

Birthday - *For young* – Poverty and falsehood.
- *For adult* – Long trouble and desolation.
- *For old* – Must execute a will.

Biscuits - Bad time ahead.

Bishop - Sorrow, grief, disappointment.

Bite - Injury from enemy.

Black - *Surroundings* – Lack of knowledge, confidence and discretion.
- *Clouds* – Troubles.
- *Painting* – Ill-health.
- *Grams* – Difficulties.

Blame - Victory over enemies.

Blanket - Prosperity may follow.

Blasphemy - *You are cursing* – Bad fortune.
- *Being cursed* – Wishes will be fulfilled.

Bleeding - *Yourself* – Malacious reports and accident.
- *Others* – Strife in life.

Blind - *Yourself* – Ill fame, sudden poverty.
- *Others* – A few real friends, someone needs you.

Blood - *To see* – Painful experiences.
- *Flowing* – Ordeal is ending.

Blood stone - Signals good health.

Blossom - Happiness to come.

Blows - *Receive* – Reconciliation with enemies.
- *Giving* – Careful of law-suit.

Blue - Truth, justice, spirituality.

Boat - *To see* – Emotions to surface.
- *To be in* – Love enters with successful ending.
- *Get in* – Gain.
- *Get out of* – Relief from worries.
- *Capsizes* – Love with tragic ending.
- *Fall in water* – Great peril.

Body - *Dead or burning* – Gain of property.

Bold - Fortune.

Bomb - Unpleasant incidents and disputes.

Bones - *To see* – Unhappiness in store for you.
- *Piles of* – Negative influences will affect you.
- *Your bones protruding* – Treachery with you.

Bonnet - *For young woman* – New lover.
- *Green or pink* – Lover will be deceitful.
- *Blue* – Lover will be true and affectionate.
- *Yellow* – Lover will be jealous.

Book keeper - Desire for advancement.

Books - *To see (for man)* – Happy future. Promotion in job.
- *To see (for women)* – Learned husband.
- *For an author* – A dream of caution.
- *Children with* – Harmony and good conduct.
- *To give* – Love and courting.
- *To take* – Meeting of friend.
- *To read* – Fame.
- *Old* – Shun evil in any form.
- *Shelves* – Need for more work.
- *Empty shelves* – Losses due to inadequate knowledge.
- *Store* – pleasure interfering with your work.

Boots - *Shining* – Important changes are likely.
- *Dirty* – Have to tolerate.
- *Untied* – Misfortune and quarrels.
- *Hurting* – Difficulties due to imprudence.

Borrowing - Sorrow, enemies to contend with.

Boss - *Happy* – Confidence and trustworthiness.
- *Annoyed* – Distrust.

Bossing - *Over others* – Elevation in rank.
- *Over you* – Difficulties.

Bottle - *Full and clear* – Legacy or gain.
- *Empty* – Financial loss. Enemies in possession of secrets.
- *Cloudy* – Unhappy incidents.
- *Drinking from* – Watch your actions.
- *Full of wine* – Prosperity.

Bouquet - Imminent social events.

Bow-arrow - *To see* – Have to be self-reliant.

- *Arrow hits a bull's eye* – Have to take decisions.
- *Arrow misses* – Disappointment in business affairs.

Bowling - Will expect a fair deal from others.

Box - *Full* – Legacy or gain.
- *Empty* – Financial loss, frustration.

Boxer - Improved health.

Boxing - Loss, enemies, unpredictable worries.

Bracelet - *To see* – Improving affairs of heart.
- *Wearing* – Marriage with wealthy person.
- *Lose* – Perplexing situation.
- *Find it* – Augurs good luck.

Brahmin - Ill-health.

Bray - Hear braying of an ass means death of an eccentric celebrity.

Bread - *To see* – Involvement in a marriage ceremony.
- *Fresh* – Signifies competence in temporal things.
- *Stale* – Illness. Uncomfortable situation.
- *Burnt* – Portends a funeral.
- *Share it* – Great happiness and joy.
- *Bake it* – Affliction.
- *Cut it from both ends* – Bad luck.

Break - *Limbs* – Sickness.
- *Table and chairs* – Insolvency.
- *Window* – Robbery. Danger from fire.
- *Looking glass* – Death of near and dear.
- *Earthenware* – Robbery by your servant.
- *Glassware* – Theft in house.
- *Wedding ring* – Death of life-partner.

Breakfast - Unsatisfactory way of living.

Breast - Elevation.

Breath - Out of breath signifies health to collapse.

Breeze - Fulfilment of desires.

Brewing - Meeting a distant friend.

Bribe - *To accept* – Dishonour.
- *To give* – Business doom.

Bride - *To see* – Marriage, profit in business.
- *Yourself* – Inheritance.
- *You kiss* – True friends.
- *Pleasure in being* – Hapiness.
- *Displeasure in being* – Disappointments.
- *Kissing others* – Health and unexpected fortune.
- *Indifferent to her husband* – Unhappiness.

Bridegroom - Broken marriage.

Bridge - *To see* – Change of luck.
- *Walking or crossing over* – Sure success.
- *Passing under* – Mighty problems.
- *Long one* – Loss of possessions and love.

Bronze - Victory, success.

Brood - *For mother* – Children will be led astray.
- *For father* – Trouble from sons.

Broom - *To see* – Constancy in marriage. Peace and contentment.
- *To lose* – Disagreements.
- *Sweeping* – Do not speculate.

Broth - Eating of broth indicates fortune.

Brother - Safety and Security and long Life.

Brush - *Hair* – Warning of carelessness.
- *Clothes* – Weighty assignment.
- *Many* – Too many interests.

Buffalo - A journey and financial security.

Bugle - *Hear* – Happy turns of events.
- *Blow* – Pleasant outcome following rough vexations.

Bugs - Confusion and complications, injury and harm from servants.

Buildings - *New* – Change of occupation and place.

- *Old* – Discord.
- *Small* – Poor performance.
- *Tall* – Success in forthcoming affairs.
- *Big* – Changes in present life.
- *Magnificent* – Long life.
- *Row of shops or factories* – New business.
- *Row of homes* – Good home life.
- *Palaces* – Wealth and honour.
- *Hotels* – Failure of hopes.
- *Skyscrapers* – Failure in plans.
- *Construct* – Gain love. Marriage.
- *Falling* – Worries.

Bull
- *To see* – Good sign for speculative activities.
- *White* – Increase in money.
- *Chasing a man* – Troubles through violent enemies.
- *Chasing a woman* – An offer of marriage.

Bulldog
- *Faithful* – Friends will come back.
- *Bites* – Injury from an enemy.

Burden - Many dependents.

Burglar
- *For man* – Difficulties in daily life.
- *For woman* – Forced sexual intrusion.
- *Overcome him/her* – You will vanquish enemies.

Burglary - Action of discredit.

Burial
- *Attending* – You will hear of marriage.
- *Pass by* – good news.
- *Own burial* – Utter frustration.

Burns - Happiness and warm friendship.

Bus
- *Sit in* – Gain of an object.
- *Miss* – Failure of plans.

Business-Calamity - Prosperity.

Butcher - Difficulties

Butter - Peace, success in love and litigation.

Butterflies - Prosperity, good news from friends.

Buttermilk - Disappointment in love.

Buttons - *To see* – Troubles will end soon.
- *Finding pearl button* – Travels.
- *Finding silver button* – Romance.
- *Finding brass button* – Invitation for a social gathering.
- *Finding wooden button* – Success after hard efforts.
- *Finding cloth covered* – Take care of your health.
- *Finding coloured button* – Unexpected pleasure.
- *Finding rusty button* – Misfortune.
- *Losing* – Anxiety over a loss.
- *Sewing* – An advancement.

Cab - *Riding in* – Secretiveness, short sickness.
- *Riding with a woman* – Complicated sexual emotions.

Cabbage - *Cutting* – Life-partner is jealous of you. Lavishness.
- *Eating* – Sickness of close one. Losses.
- *Green* – Unfaithfulness and infidelity.

Cabin - *Ships cabin* – Warns of enemies. Trouble in marriage.
- *Locked cabin* – Good luck after hard work.

Cackle - Hearing the cackle of ducks means poverty.

Cage - *To see* – Involvement in law suits.
- *Bird(s) in* – Agreeable marriage.
- *Letting a bird escape* – Elopement.

Cake - *To see* – Involvement in a marriage ceremony.
- *Wedding* – Bad luck.
- *Spicy* – Approaching marriage.
- *To eat* – Health.

Calamity - Prosperity.

Calendar - Make calculations carefully.

Calf - A happy married life.

Called - *Man (hearing) being called* – Second marriage, beware of second wife.
- Woman (hearing) being called-Lust.

Calm - Reconciliation with separated friends.

Calumny - Respect and honour.

Camel - Revenge from opponents. Profit and promotion.

Camera - *For man* – Trust the one you love.
- *For woman* – Very pleasant experience.

Camp - *To see* – Keep a firm control on your temper.
- *Camping* – Need to travel.
- *Military* – News of wedding.

Campaign - You will be called upon to nurse a close one.

Canal - *Muddy water* – Injury at home or in business.
- *Clear water* – Happiness and prosperity.

Canary - This bird presages comfortable habitation.

Cancer - Health and strength.

Candle - *Lighted* – Signifies joyous occasions.
- *Blown out* – Death in close circle.
- *For girl* – Proposal of marriage.

Candy - *Receive box of* – Financial improvement.
- *From women* – Adoration from the sender.
- *Sending box of* – Face disappointment.
- *Making* – Expect a new adventure.

Cane - *Carry it* – Increased wealth.
- *Drop it* – Be careful in all of your undertakings.
- *Pointing it to someone* – Sexual desire.
- *Break it* – Bad luck.
- *Sugar* – Happiness.

Canker - *In son's mouth* – Son will be an eloquent speaker.
- *In daughter's mouth* – She will be a singer/actress.

Cannon - Death or illness in the family.

Canoe - *Paddling in calm waters* – Ability to run business.
- *Paddling in shallow waters* – Brief happiness.

Canopy - Change of residence to cheaper place.

Cap - Beware of vanity and pride.

Cape - *Wearing* – To take semblance of authority.
- *Girl seeing it* – Will be protected by an older man.

Captain - *To see* – Noble aspirations.
- *To be one* – Desire to command.

Captive - Insolvency. Imprisonment, unhappy marriage.

Captured - Warning of marital troubles

Car - *To see* – Financial prosperity.
- *Broken* – Get yourself medically checked up.
- *You drive* – You are in control.
- *To be in* – You are a subordinate.

Cardinal - *Is a bird* – Urge for freedom and relieving responsibilities.
- *Is a clergy* – Desire to overcome wrong.

Cards - *To see* – In love, which will materialize in marriage.
- *Playing* – Realization of your plans or marriage.
- *Gambling* – May face economical strain.
- *If a loser* – You have made enemies.
- *More diamonds* – Wealth. Ill-tempered partner.
- *More spades* – Bad news.
- *More hearts* – Fidelity of a loved one.
- *More clubs* – Money by marriage.

Carnival - *To see* – Advent of an unusal entertainment.
- *Performing* – Many changes.

Carpenter - Beware of friends and avoid all schemes and plans.

Carpet - *To see* – A sign of good luck.
- *Walking on* – Portends luxurious living.
- *Cleaning it* – Personal affairs need attention.
- *Buying or selling* – Commerical involvement.

Carriage - Betokens poverty

Carrots - Gains and success.

Cart - You may be falsely accused or blamed.

Castle - *To see* – Good health.
- *Being in* – Legacy. Ambitions fulfilled.

- *Old and dilapidated* – Disappointment.
- *Living in* – Vast riches and holdings.
- *Leaving it* – Losses.

Cat - To see portends bad luck and treachery.
- *Black* – Death in family.
- *Domestic* – Your intuition will help you.

Caterpillars - Troubles through secret enemies.

Cathedral - Take care of your health and not to worry. Travel.

Cattle - Happiness in love, affluence.

Cauliflower - *Eating* – Sickness.
- *See growing* – Prosperity.

Cave - Beware of your enemies and friends.

Cellar - *Being in* – Gains and success.
- *Damp* – Property losses. Lack of self-confidence.
- *Empty* - Poverty.
- *Wine cellar for man* – Business offer to arrive.
- *Wine cellar for girl* – Betrothal with gambler.

Cemetry - Happiness in store. Fame.

Chaff - Faulty schemes which will prove abortive.

Chain - *To see* – Engagement for unmarried.
- *Tied with* – Temporary setback and fame.
- *Freeing from* – Overcome obstacles.

Chair - *To see* – Success.
- *Empty* – Heavy obligation.
- *Occupied* – Illness or accident.

Chamber - *For young girl* – Love against parent's wishes.
- *For man* – Business transactions.

Champion - *Yourself* – Desire to assert yourself.

Chapel - Disappointments.

Chappals (Indian footwear) - Good event in house.

Charity - *For richman* – Loss of fortune.
- *For a lady* – Bestow her affections on an unworthy person.

Chased - *Being* – Face the fear and fight.

Chastise - Obedient and docile children.

Chattering - Gain of good position.

Cheating - *To see* – Loss of money.
- *Being victim* – A few royal friends.
- *Others* – Reward for honesty.

Checkers - *Playing* – Attainment of ambition.
- *Losing* – Expect obstacles.
- *Watching* – Expect contentment.

Cheeks - Meeting with opposite sex.

Cheese - Pay no attention to rumours.

Cheque - Beware of extravagance. Control your finance.

Cherries - *To see* – Good luck.
- *To eat* – Wishes materialize.
- *Green* – Promise of fortune.

Chess - *Playing* – Fall out with friends.
- *Win* – Gain advantage over enemies.
- *Lose* – Enemies will have upper hand.
- *Watching* – Unfaithful loved ones.

Chest - Disease. Infatuation.

Chest Nuts - *For unmarried woman* – Will be courted.
- *For married woman* – Sickness.

Chickens - Impending change, worries. Concentrated planning.

Children - Success and happiness. Removal of worries.

Choking - *Yourself* – Fear of someone in real life.
- *Other* – Hatred of the person.

Cholera - Accident.

Church - *To see* – Fulfilment of hopes.
- *Entering* – Marriage vows, wedding.

- *Coming out* – Protection.
- *Far away* – Disappointment.

Churning - Prosperity, happy marriage. Good crops.

Cinema - A good sign for those in love.

Circus - End of worries.

City
- *To see* – Meeting with woman.
- *To run from* – Happiness, Gain.
- *Barren* – Journey. Worries.

Clap - Happiness.

Clergy - Desire to overcome wrong.

Climbing
- *Ladder* – Setbacks but eventual success.
- *Stairs* – Aspirations are achievable.
- *Hills* – Sexual desires fulfilled.
- *Mountains* – Ambitions fulfilled.
- *Elevators* – Overcome exhaustion.
- *Reach top* – Surmount all troubles.

Clock
- *To see* – Fear of losing a job.
- *Strikes* – Fear of self-death or of a close relative.
- *Not working* – Good news. Pregnancy of wife.

Clothes
- *Wear new* – Poverty. Difficulties.
- *Wear old* – Good fortune.
- *Wear black* – Grief.
- *Having plenty* – Shortage of clothes.
- *Having few* – Will have enough clothes.
- *Buying* – Success in love.
- *Making* – Birth of a child.
- *New* – Prosperity.
- *Soiled* – Deceitful action.
- *Torn* – Need to be cautious in dealings.
- *Partly dressed* – Prosperity.
- *No clothes on* – Financial gains.

Clouds - Promotion. Good health. Escape from difficulties.

Coach - Troubles.

Coal - *Burning bright* – Money to come.
- *To see* – Bad luck.

Coat - *Wear new* – Unexpected honours.
- *Wear borrowed* – Crisis will force you to borrow.
- *Lose one* – Avoid speculations.

Cobra - Success all around.

Cock - *Hear a rooster* – Good day.
- *Hear in morning* – Good omen.
- *Hear in night* – Forebodes sorrows.
- *See fighting* – Family quarrels.

Cocktails - Refrain from exaggeration and deception.

Coffee - *Self-drinking* – Happiness. Settlement.
- *Other drinking* – Unhappiness due to talkativeness.

Coffin - *To see* – Bad luck. Bad debts.
- *You in* – Failure in business. Loss of job.
- *Moved by* – Sickness and death.
- *Of young* – Death of loved one.

Coins - *Copper* – Heavy responsibilities.
- *Nickel* – Unhappy days ahead.
- *Silver* – Prosperity.
- *Gold* – Prosperous times. Travels.

Collar - *Wearing a tight collar* – Fear of powerful person.
- *Woman putting on a collar* – Engagement.

College - *To see* – Achieve an ambition.
- *Attending* – Gain fame in profession.

Colours - *Black* – Evil.
- *Blue* – Purity.
- *Brown* – Money. Luck.
- *Green* – Intuition. Fruitfulness. Travels.
- *Gray* – Period of "Marking time."
- *Orange* – Delays and hurdles.
- *Yellow* – Setbacks and struggles

	- *Red* – Passion or sinfulness.
	- *Pale puce* – An over-fanciful imagination.
Comb	- *Your hair* – Illness of a friend or loved one.
Combat	- *To see* – Rivalry. Desire for revenge.
	- *Win* – Will retain affection of your lover.
Comets	- War. Famine. Misfortune.
Command	- *Others command* – Anger.
	- *You command* – Rise in life.
Companion	- Abiding friendship.
Compass	- Prosperity through friends.
Complaint	- Everything in order.
Complexion	- *Good* – Sickness.
	- *Bad* – Health.
Concert	- Good time. Artistic endeavour.
Concubine	- Immorality.
Confectionery	- Trouble due to sudden illness in family.
Confetti	- Work before playing.
Conjurer	- Desire to display latent talents.
Consumption	- Having this lingering disease forebodes long life.
Convent	- *For man* – Desire to get away from responsibilities.
	- *For young girls* Disillusionment and despair.
Convention	- *To attend* – Gains.
Convicted	- Troubles.
Cooking	- *To see* – Avoid gossip. Happy marriage.
	- *Yourself* – Desire to please someone.
Copper	- Spiritual thinking.
Corks	- *Corking bottles* – will have to throw a party.
	- *Uncorking bottles* – A friend will be visiting.
Corn	- Health and wealth. Speculations shall bring prosperity.

Corpse - *To see* – Death or termination of task.
- *Yourself* – Desire to escape troubles.
- *For business man* – Loss of reputation.
- *For young person* – Disappointment in love.

Cot - Meeting with opposite sex.

Cotton - Poor wages.

Cough - Will have strong chest and lungs.

Country - *Beautiful and fertile* – Wealth and prosperity.
- *Dry and bare* – Trouble to come.

Courting - A worrying love affair.

Cover - Wearing white, black or red cloth forebodes misfortune/death.

Cow - *To see* – Promotion.
- *Milking* – Prosperity in business.
- *Being chased by* – An enemy.
- *Escapes the chase* – Victory over an enemy.

Cowslips - Sudden change of fortunes.

Crabs - Danger of shipwreck and drowning.

Cradle - *Empty* – Presages sickness. Sense of insecurity.
- *Broken* – Illness of youngest child.
- *Baby in* – Marital happiness.
- *Rocking* – Many difficulties.
- *Rock itself* – Death of mother.
- *Twins in* – Financial gains.

Crape - Wearing crape foretells marriage of an old friend.

Crawling - Difficulties.

Cremation Ground - Bad health.

Crew - A friend will be facing shipwreck.

Cricket - *To play* – Difficult time ahead.
- *To watch* – Disease and illness.

Cries - *Of distress* – Good news from a friend.

- *Of joy* – Death of relative.
- *Of despair* – Gain by speculation.

Criminal
- *Associated with* – Unscrupulous dealings.
- *Yourself* – You have infringed upon the rights of others.

Crocodile - Enemies. Opponents. Troubles.

Cross
- *To see* – Troubles foreshadowed.
- *Person bearing it* – You will be called for charities.

Crow
- *To see* – Loss. Ill-health. Funeral.
- *To catch* – Over committing.
- *To shoot* – Harm from enemies.
- *Crowing* – Meeting with friends.

Crowd - Try to understand and help your friends.

Crown
- *To see* – Respect and gain.
- *Wear a royal crown* – Degradation.
- *Give a crown* – Will rise to independence.

Cruel-Animals
- *To see* – enmity.
- *Biting of* – Difficulties.
- *Killing* – Success over enemies.

Crutches
- *Walking on* – Unfavourable.
- *Other man with* – Injury to the man.

Crying - *Dream of crying* – Good times ahead.

Crystal - Ruin and downfall of loved ones.

Cuckoo
- *To see* – Good fortune.
- *To hear* – No success in love and business.

Cucumbers - Health for sick. Agreeable marriage for single.

Curd
- *To see* – Good fortune.
- *To eat* – Gain from an establishment.

Currants - Happiness. Success. Love for sweatheart.

Curtains
- *Opening/Closing/Pulling* – Fever, illness.
- *Soiled* – Moral disgrace.

Cut
- *To see* – Sickness.
- *With scissors* – Undesirable debate.

Cutting - *To see* – Emotional fear.
- *Someone* – You mistrust the person.
- *Oneself* – Desire to escape strains of work problem.

Cycle - A journey.

Dacoits - Loss through accidents.

Dagger - *Seen by man* – Anxiety and fear resulting in impotence.
- *Seen by woman* – Fear of gossip and slander.
- *Seen by juniors* – Should remain faithful to your love.
- *Snatching from assailant* – Fears will not materialize.

Dairy - Secular concern. Marriage with homely person.

Daisy - *To see* – Good health and Security.
- *White* – Bring love.
- *Black-eyed* – Jealousy.

Damsel - Worries and grief.

Dancing - Happiness and conviviality. Love forthcoming.

Danger - Be careful.

Dark Night - *To see* – Worries.
- *To emerge from* – Will regain your reputation.

Daughter - *To see* – Happiness of son.
- *Birth of* – Happy news.

Dead - *To see* – Disappointments. Sorrow.
- *Talking to* – Name and fame.
- *Demanding from* – Grief. Loss.
- *Seeing elders* – Success. Gain of money.
- *Carrying dead* – Gain of money. Happiness.
- *Weeping dead* – Freedom from worries.
- *Laughing dead* – Worries. Separation.

Dead Body - *Covered* – Wealth, health and happiness.
- *Naked* – Relief from vices.

Death - *To hear of* – Bad news from a friend.
- *Of self* – Good days are coming.
- *Of wife* – Birth of twins.

- *Of child* – Inauspicious.
- *Of friend* – Good news.
- *Of stranger* – Good omen.
- *Of a sick* – Portends death.

Debt - *Yourself in* – Prosperity.
- *Capable of paying* – Losses in business.

Decorations - Honour is in store for you.

Deer - Expect changes.

Defecate - Get wealth.

Defraud - Will face character assassination.

Delicate - Strength and robustness.

Delight - Sorrow and trouble from an unexpected source.

Demand - Beware of friends.

Dentist - Worries ahead, but they will pass away.

Desert - Love is just round the corner. Journey.

Despair - Will soon have cause to rejoice.

Dejective - Life without blemish upon your character.

Devil - Susceptibility to flattery and temptation.

Devotion - Temporal happiness.

Diadem - Wearing a diadem signifies degradation.

Diamond - Love marriage, prosperity.

Dice - Changes in business and environment.

Difficulties - Promotion.

Digging - *Clean ground* – Thrift and good luck.
- *Dirty or wet ground* – Troubles.
- *For gold and find it* – Good fortune.
- *Get nothing* – Disappointments.
- *For water* – Happiness.

Dining - *With officers* – Long life.

Dinner - *Eating* – Expect invitations for parties.
- *Preparing* – Happy home life.

Dirt - *On yourself* – Sickness and sorrow.
- *Someone is throwing* – Defamation.

Disaster - *Hear of* – Exaltation of some kind.
- *At sea* – Prosperous voyage.

Disco Party - *To see* – Difficulties.
- *To join* – Trauma.

Disease - *Yourself diseased* – Early recovery.
- *For young* – Beware of evil company and intemperance.

Disgrace - Will act prudently and gain favour and reputation.

Dishes - *You break* – Loss.

Dispute - Will surmount every trial.

Distance - *You are at* – Family quarrels.
- *Others at* – Will receive communication from them.

Ditch - *To see* – Scandal in love affairs.
- *Fall in* – Loss of virtue, integrity and temptation.
- *To jump over* – Will narrowly escape public fury.

Diving - Do not hesitate in your action. Meeting a friend.

Divorce - Wedding and sign of fidelity of partner.

Docks - News from across the sea.

Doctor - *To see* – Be sure of good health.
- *To visit* – Will have a discouraging situation.
- *You are* – Latent desire for power or authority.

Dog - *To see* – Be sure of luck and success.
- *Barking* – Overcome difficulties.
- *Bite* – Troubles, fear of opponent.
- *Wagging tail* – A happy time.
- *Bites you* – A friend will turn into foe.
- *Growling* – Resentment and depression.
- *Baying* – Separation from loved ones or death.
- *White* – Means marriage for young lady, business for man.

- *Black* – Task will be abandoned.
- *Police* – Fear, guilt or desire for protection.

Doll
- *For child* – Indicates loneliness.
- *For grown-up* – Desire for protection.

Dolphins
- Shipwreck, loss of life, or liability.

Dominoes
- *Winning game* – Desire for adulation, and expenses.
- *Losing game* – Bad name for persons you love.

Donkey
- *To see* – End of troubles.
- *Child seeing it* – Desire to have friends.
- *Hear bray of* – Release from unpleasant connections.
- *Leading it* – Feeling to get extricated.
- *Riding* – Sensual desires. Rise in life.
- *Being kicked* – Sexual impulses. Enemy harms.

Door
- *To open* – Portends success.
- *To unlock* – Success.
- *To see* – Worries.
- *Locked* – Danger.
- *Falling* – Discord.
- *Closed* – Loss of happiness.
- *People entering and leaving* – Loss of money due to mismanagement.

Dove
- *To see* – Be sure of peace and contentment.
- *Hear it* – Death of a dear friend.
- *Shot and fall* – Own death.

Dragon
- Sudden change.

Dream
- *A dream within your dream* – Advancement.

Dress
- *Putting on* – Lucky for lovers.
- *Buying* – Advancement.
- *White* – Happiness.
- *Red* – Disputes.
- *Black* – Worries.

Drink
- Downfall.

Drinking
- *Water* – Gain from king.

- *Milk* – Fame and honour.
- *Woman's milk* – Loss.
- *Dairy Milk* – Good health.
- *Curd* – Fame.
- *Wine* – Financial gain.
- *Poison* – Change of profession.
- *Oil* – Ill-luck. Loss.
- *Medicine* – Recovery of health.
- *Getting toxicated* – Shirking responsibilities.

Driving - *To see* – Be careful in business and social sphere.
- *Yourself* – Desire for independence.
- *Others* – You can trust that person.

Drizzle - Happiness.

Dropsy - Insanity. Suicide.

Drowning - *To see* – Fear of exhaustion under pressure.
- *Self* – Loss. Blemish on character.
- *Escape* – Getting rid of troubles.

Drum - *Hear* – Worries.

Drunk - *Self* – Desire to get rid of responsibility.
- *Others* – Irresponsible dependant.

Ducks - *Flying* – Riches.
- *Swimming* – Good for merchants and artisans.

Dumb - Of being dumb means demean yourself.

Dung hill - Prosperity. Marriage of choice.

Dust - *To see* – journey.
- *Covering you* – Loss in business.
- *Covering a woman* – She will be deserted.
- *Being blind with* – Dispersion of family.
- *Remove it* – Recover your former state.

Dwarf - *To see* – Favourable sign. Elevation in rank.
- *Yourself* – Helplessness.

Dye - *Dyeing clothes* – Change in lifestyle.

Dying - *Self* – Sense of guilt or problem.

- *Other person* – Remove him/her far away.

Eagles
- *To see flying* – Desires will be fulfilled.
- *High in sky* – Prosperity in profession.
- *In cage* – Downfall through enemies' plot.
- *On a church* – Fortune beyond seas.
- *To kill* – Frustration and failure.

Ear
- Beware of gossip and an evil person.

Earrings
- *To see* – Good news.
- *To put on* – Financial loss.
- *Broken* – Malicious propaganda.

Earth
- *To dream of* – Loss of a friend.
- *Lying on* – Death of a person.
- *Black* – Sorrow.
- *Kissing* – Humiliation.
- *Eating* – Illness.
- *Under it* – Disaster.
- *Quake* – Upheaval in the life.
- *Filled with grains* – Good luck.
- *Pastures* – Good children.
- *Being buried in* – Wealth.

Earthquake
- *To see* – Destruction. War.
- *To feel* – Business failure and distress.

Eatables
- *Fill in bag* – Profit.
- *Selling* – Loss and disrespect.

Eating
- *Alone* – Loss and melancholy.
- *With others* – Personal gain.
- *Platter being taken away in midway* – Troubles.
- *Others* – Good luck.
- *Mango, grapes* – Respect, gains.
- *Human flesh* – Unexpected gains.
- *Halwa* – Long life, comforts.
- *Meat* – Gain of money.
- *Bread* – Gain of object.

- *Honey, rice* – Fulfilment of an ambition.
- *In party* – Gain of wealth.
- *Onions* – Happiness, but also disrespect.
- *Sweets* – Promotion, respect.
- *Fish* – Meeting a beautiful woman.
- *Bitter thing* – Troubles.
- *Endlessly* – Worries and restless living.
- *Lion's meat* – gain of wealth.
- *Apple* – Birth of son.
- *Food* – Domestic quarrels.
- *Vegetables* – Gain of money.
- *Potatoes* – Good health.
- *Almonds* – Gain of wealth.
- *Betel leaves* – Meeting with beloved.

Eclipse - *Moon* – Disease and worries.
- *Sun* – Birth of son.

Education - Advance in literary fame.

Egg - An unexpected gain.

Electricity - Good luck.

Elephant - *To see* – Success in your undertakings but go slow.
- *To ride on* – Promotion. Fame.

Elevator - *Ascending* – Desire for advancement. Material gain.
- *Descending* – Discouragement.

Elopement - Sudden and unexpected gains and difficulties.

Embrace - *To see* – Quarrels and bitterness is presaged.
- *Beloved* – Faithful and happy.
- *A lover* – Sexual relation.
- *A friend* – Longing to help others.
- *Man* – Deceitful friend.
- *Woman* – Misfortune.
- *Being embraced* – Travel.

Embroidery - Success through careful planning.

Emerald - Purchasing of it signifies grief.

Employer - *Meeting with* – Chance to prove your ability.
- *Unhappy* – Distrust with him.

Employment - *Want it* – Prosperity.
- *Give it* – Will injure employees.

Enemy - *To see* – Success over obstacles.
- *Talk to* – Be careful.
- *Apologises* – Success over them.
- *You beat* – Favourable.
- *He beats* – Misfortune.

Engagement - Presages your own or a friends' engagement.

Engine - *To see* – Desire to display power.
- *To drive* – Emotional urge to impress others.

Engineer - Motivation for discharge of duties.

Enlist - Enlisting into army denotes better employment.

Entertainment - Joyful festivity. Safety in battle.

Envelope - Unexpected news.

Envy - *Being envied* – Will be admired and loved.
- *Others* – Bad luck.

Ermine - Honour and dignity.

Escalator - *Ascending* – Material gains.
- *Descending* – Depression.

Escape - *An accident* – Improvement in status.
- *Confinement* – Happiness.
- *Fail to* – Gossip and slander.

Estate - *For young woman* – Will marry a lazy and worthless man.
- *For men* – Misery.

Evening - An early death.

Evil spirits - Difficulties.

Examination - Failing to live up to expectation.

Excrement - *To see* – Gain of wealth.
- *To eat* – Find treasure.
- *To touch* – Get enormous wealth.
- *To defecate* – Get wealth.

Execution - *Of self* – Guilt complex.
- *Of others* – Desire to overthrow the authority.

Exhibition - Success through social activities.

Exile - Long travel.

Explosion - A big event of your life is about to happen.

Eye - *To see* – Surprise awaits you. Enemies are scheming.
- *Sore* – Sickness or deception.
- *Squint* – Loss in some enterprises.
- *Defective vision* – Disappointment.
- *To lose an eye* – Trouble.
- *To meet one-eyed person* – Big loss and trouble.
- *Brown* – Deceit and perfidy.
- *Blue* – Shilly-Shally outlook.
- *Grey* – Fondness for flattery.

Eyebrows - Hard hurdles.

Face - *Own face in glass* – Your secret plans will surface.
- *Bright* – Favourable.
- *Ugly/disfigured* – Troubles.
- *Old* – Breaking up of an association.

Factory - Will receive a business offer.

Faeces - *Human* – Money or wealth.
- *Animal* – Material gain.

Failure - Success.

Fair - Good time in offing.

Fairy - Meeting with a fairy means recovery from disease.

Faithful - Test for success.

Falcon - Foe injuring you with tongue and mind.

Fall - Loss of property. Stormy voyage.

Falling - *To see* – Symbol of fear.
- *Oneself* – Loss of power and control.
- *To ground* – Death warning.
- *In well* – Worries.
- *From balcony* – Check weak areas of your house.
- *From wall* – Reversal in rank.
- *From height* – Loss. Diffculties.
- *You are hurt* – You are neglecting basics.
- *Of teeth* – Long life. Good health.
- *In love* – Out of favour. Down.

Fame - Failure.

Famine - National prosperity. Individual comfort.

Fan - Troubles in matter of heart. Good news.

Farewell - Changes in business.

Farm - Peace and happiness. Desire for security.

Fasting - Escape from trouble.

Fat - Illness and fever.

Father - *To see* – Wishes will come true. Good time.
- *To kill* – Signifies repression.

Fawn - Young deer in dreams foretells inconstancy between lovers.

Fear - Someone is trying for your downfall.

Feasting - Disappointments. Enemies.

Feathers - Be on the look out for troubles.

Feeding - Good news.

Feet - Whatever frightens you will not happen.

Fence - *Encircled by* – Emotional restraint or denial.
- *Climb over* – Will surmount problem.
- *Creep under* – Will commit a degrading act.
- *Knock it* – Happy times.
- *For young woman* – Desire for marriage and motherhood.

Festival - Sadness, sickness, sorrow.

Fiddle - Prosperity and enjoyment.

Fields - *Green* – Prosperity.
- *Withered or scorched* – Poverty.
- *Barley* – Wealth.
- *Wheat* – Agreeable connection.
- *Newly ploughed* – Success awaits you.

Fight - Beware of jealous and treacherous friends.

Fighting - Will be successful in spite of difficulties.

Figs - Prosperity. Happiness. Legacy.

Figures - Financial changes.

Fingers - *Soiled* – Troubles.
- *Scratched* – Sufferings.
- *Cut* – Injury is likely.

Fire - *To see* – Advised to destroy painful memory.
- *House on* – Warning of friction and/or disharmonous life.
- *Home on* – Loving family, friends and servants.
- *Store on* – Expansive business, gains.
- *Shop on* – Increased income.
- *Village/town on* – Social status.
- *Crops burning* – Loss.
- *Aftermath of* – Many vexing situations.
- *You falling in* – Misfortune.
- *You are burnt* – Ruining business.
- *You fighting with* – Troubles and worries.
- *Firemen fighting with* – Good news is on the way.
- *Without smoke* – Recovery from poor health.
- *Smoke only* – Disappointments.
- *Flames* – Prosperity.
- *Kindling* – Pleasant surprises.
- *Baking in* – Profit in business.
- *Warming hands* – Lucrative work.

- *Lifting fire* – Troubles.

Firing - *Pistol/Revolver* – Steady rise in life.
- *Gun* – Delayed rise in life.
- *Missile* – Sharp rise in life.

Fish - *To see* – Happiness to follow. Spiritual growth.
- *In water* – Unexpected favours.
- *Dead* – Losses.

Fisherman - Spiritual enlightenment.

Fishing - Good luck and riches.

Fits - Health and happiness.

Flag - A journey abroad. Peace of mind.

Flame - Happy home life.

Flies - Beware of insincere persons around you. Ill health.

Flight - Discredit.

Floating - *In air* — Will achieve personal acclaim.
- *On water* – Fortune and long life.
- *Sink in* – Poverty.

Flood - Good affairs, financial gains.

Flour - Sickness or death of a near friend.

Flowers - *To see* – A wedding in the family. Meeting lover.
- *White* – Comforts.
- *Red* – Respect. Promotion.
- *Rose* – Promotion.
- *Growing* – Pleasure and happy working condition.
- *Withered* – Disappointments, regrets.
- *To gather* – A surprise.
- *In a bouquet* – Social events.

Flute - *To hear* – Many friends and security.
- *To play* – Artistic honours.

Fly - *In aeroplane* – Success in business.

Flying - *To see* – Desire to escape from problems.
- *Yourself* – Great joy.

	- *In sky* – Death of a dear one.
	- *To escape* – Will get rid of problems.
	- *With black wings* – Disappointments.
	- *With white wings* – Excellent business prospects.
Fog	- Will come out of a trouble safely.
Food	- *To see* – Good fortune.
	- *Bad/ spoiled* – Difficulties around you.
	- *Eating* – Greed.
	- *Eating with others* – Social awkwardness.
Football	- You are going to be very busy.
Forest	- *To see* – Good omen.
	- *Be in* – Loss in trade.
	- *Being lost in* – Your troubles will end soon.
	- *Alone and afraid* – Losses.
	- *Alone and happy in* – New home.
	- *For literary person* – Fame and name.
	- *Green* – Happiness expected.
	- *Appealing* – Prosperity and pleasure.
Fort	- Self-reliant. Strong. Promotion.
Fortress	- *Confined in* – Undue influence of others.
	- *Confine others* – Enrichment for you.
Fortune	- Poverty.
Fountain	- *Overflowing and clean* – Freedom from want.
	- *Muddy* – Troubles.
Fowls	- Moderate comforts. Rivalry for lovers.
Fox	- Cunningness to manifest.
Fracticide	- Being guilty of this crime denotes failure.
Fraud	- *Committed by you* – Public appreciation.
	- *By others* – They would have robbed you.
Friend	- *Good* – Happy love affairs.
	- *A happy* – Prosperity for him/her.
	- *A haggered* – Distress for him/her.

- *Unfaithful* – Faithful and true.
- *At distance and happy* – Good news.
- *At distance and alarming* – Evil has befallen them.
- *In bright red dress* – Anxiety and implication.
- *In darkness* – Trouble for him/her and you.
- *In animal form* – Enemies will take on you.
- *Like a statue* – Fast advancement.
- *Death of* – Good news.

Frightened
- *Yourself* – Joy.
- *Terrorised* – Bliss.
- *Pained* – Pleasure.
- *Black mailed* – Will be successful.
- *Overcome fear* – Legacy of wealthy person.

Frogs
- Will be vexed by petty annoyance. Promotion. Good crops. Business expansion.

Frost
- *For man* – Trials and troubles.
- *For woman* – Danger of sensual man.

Frown
- Good friends and company.

Fruits
- *To see* – Financial gain.
- *Almonds* – Loss of liberty, deceit in love, difficulties.
- *Apples* – Long life. Faithful sweet heart. Riches by trade.
- *Apricot* – Prosperity. A speedy marriage. Dutiful children.
- *Cherries* – Disappointment in love. Vexation in married life.
- *Currant* – Happiness in life. Success in undertakings.
- *Elder berries* – Riches. Success in business. Good crops.
- *Figs* – Prosperity. Happiness. Legacy.
- *Filberts* – Anger. Trouble. Decay of trade. Prison.
- *Goose berries* – Many children, More sons. Accomplishment.
- *Grapes* – Cheerful companion. Success in trade.
- *Lemons* – Uneasiness on account of children.

Disappointment in love.
- *Medlars* – Riches. Defeat to enemies in lawsuit.
- *Melons* – Speedy recovery for sick. Harmony.
- *Mulberries* – Happy marriage. Ominous to farmers.
- *Nuts* – Riches. Troublesome undertakings.
- *Orange* – Loss of goods and reputation. Attacks.
- *Peaches* – Love is reciprocated. Riches. Good crops.

Funeral - A wedding, perhaps your own.

Fur - A rich life partner.

Furniture - A happy sign for those engaged.

Future - Control your activities.

Gala - A travel to distant places.

Galloping - *Horse* – Unexpected news.

Gallows - Much trade. Much money and honour. A high position.

Gambling - Be careful in your new deals.

Games - *To see* – Expect contentment.
- *Playing* – Attainment of ambition.
- *Losing* – Expect obstacles.

Gang - *Attacked by* – Desire for sex or union.

Ganges-River - Happiness for remaining life.

Garden - *To see* – A happy and contended future. Gain through women.
- *Evergreen* – Peace and comfort.
- *Of vegetables* – Misery and calumny.
- *Walking through* – Happiness.

Garland - Favourable time.

Garret - Expect a gift.

Garter - *Lose* – Uncomfortable life.
- *Returned by lover* – Strength of affection.

Gate - *To See* – Opportunity. Enlightenment.

- *Open* – You will get over your difficulties.
- *Closed* – No immediate chance of success.
- *Broken* – Failures.
- *Swinging on* – Pleasure before work.

Gather - *Money* – Improvement in your state.
- *Fruit in season* – Enjoyment, health and happiness.
- *Fruit out of season* – Grief. Deceitful love.

Gems - Success in love. Pilgrimage.

Ghee - Relief from troubles.

Ghost - Benefits to come. Watch your relatives.

Gift - *To receive* – Check your finances. Good fortune.
- *To send* – Desire for attention or flattery.

Gipsy - Travels are indicated (life of Gypsy).

Girl - Happiness in near future.

Glass - *Looking* – Do not be too sure of yourself.

Gleaning - Rise in life.

Gloomy - Will be cheerful and in high spirits.

Gloves - *Wear new* – Warning to be economical.
- *Wear old* – Deceit by others.
- *Find* – New love interest.
- *Lose* – Look for new interest. Change of abode.

Goal - Increase in honour.

Goat - Beware of enemies around you. Bonus.

God - Afflicted and about to die.

Gold - *To feel* – Comforts.
- *To see* – May expect a gift.
- *Biscuits* – Worries. Loss.
- *Ornaments* – Success. Fortune.
- *Bracelets* – Gain of property.
- *Find* – Anxiety to realize ambitions.
- *Lose* – Have suffered negligence.
- *Touch* – Look for a new hobby.

Goose - Wishes will be granted. May receive good news.

Goose-berries - *To see* – Desire to evade an issue.
- *Picking* – Be optimist.

Gore - Dreadful death.

Gown - Loss of clothes.

Grain - Industry. Perseverance and wealth.

Gramo-phone - Expect a change in your life.

Grand-parents - *Meeting* – Difficulties.
- *Conversing* – Follow their advice.

Grapes - *To see* – Happiness. Cheerful companion.
- *To see hanging* – will attain eminent positions.
- *Eating* – Hardships.
- *Plucking* – Realization of desires.
- *Doubting the quality* – Fears of success.
- *Poisoned* – Worries and fears.

Grass - *To see green* – Higher position.
- *Walking on* – Profit.
- *Gathering* – Journey. Happy union.
- *Withered* – Sickness and distress.

Grave - *To see* – Gainful property.
- *New* – Unfortunate omen.
- *Opened* – Dissolution of close one.
- *Dig* – Evading punishment for your sin.
- *Yourself in* – Happiness.
- *Other person in* – Disagreement with him.

Gravy - *Eating* – Failing health and disappointing business.

Grease - *Be in* – Enjoyable journeys.

Green - Simplicity. Natural. Maturity.

Grief - Promotion.

Groans - *Hearing painful* – Mysterious disappearance of a friend.

Ground - *Digging* – Worries.
- *Burial* – Deceit.
- *Noise* – Gain of an object.
- *Falling upon* – Dishonour. Shame. Grief.

Guest - A holiday trip.

Guitar - Respect. Comforts.

Gun - *To see* – Quarrels with friends and relatives.
- *To hear* – Loss of employment. Slander. Mismanagement.
- *Being shot* – Sexual impulse.
- *You shoot* – Foreshadows dishonour.
- *For a maid* – Ill reputation.
- *For married woman* – Unhappiness through other women.

Gutter - Immorality. Forebodes unhappiness.

Gymnast - Misfortune in speculation or trade.

Gypsy - *To see* – Wish for change of fortune, travels.
- *Dancing* – Desire for emotional outlet.
- *Reading your fortune* – Dissatisfaction.
- *Visiting a camp of* – Importance and disadvantage.

Haggard - Pleasant news from friends far away.

Hail - Hailing or snowing denotes bleak prospects, poor crop.

Hail Storm - Difficulties.

Hair - *For woman* – Carelessness.
- *For man* – Neurosis.
- *Hair-cut* – Clearance of debt.
- *Seeing one's own white* – Long life. Good health.
- *Turning grey* – Death and contagion in families.
- *Turning white* – Sudden calamity and grief.
- *Growing soft and luxuriant* – Happiness and luxury.
- *Comparing a white with black* – Distressing fortune.
- *Combing* – Relief from disease.
- *Well kept* – Fortune will improve.

- *Tangled* – Domestic troubles.
- *Falling off* – Relief from debt and worries.
- *Ladies hair* – Worries. Unrest.
- *Red* – Changes.

Hair-dresser - Undisturbed routine.

Haj - Going to Haj indicates fructification of hopes.

Halter - Round the neck of an animal – Position of distinction.

Hammer - Hard work desired for success.

Ham - Happy domestic circle.

Hand
- *To see* – Meet a relation. Financical gain.
- *Well formed* – Distinction and steep rise.
- *Malformed* – Disappointments and poverty.
- *Beautiful* – Distinction will be achieved.
- *Holding hands* – Emotional strain.
- *Admiring* – Woman will be enticed into illicit engagement.
- *Shaking* – Realization of hopes.
- *Enlarging* – Progress in your activities.
- *Shortening* – Reverses.
- *Washing* – Participate in joyous festivity.
- *Tied* – Too much restraint.
- *Handcuffed* – Difficulties and troubles.
- *Dirty* – Beware of wrong doing.
- *Blood on* – Estrangement.
- *Injured* – Enemy succeeds.
- *Detached* – Isolation.
- *Hairy* – Sordid imaginings.
- *Handling fire* – High and commanding position.
- *Burnt* – Loss by ego.

Handcuffs
- *To see* – Rigid ties that are unbearable.
- *To break open* – Mental incarceration will be removed.

Handkerchief - Business rivalry.

Handsome - Will be stricken with an infectious disorder.

Hand-writing - Of a dead friend warns you to improve.

Hanging - *Being hanged* – Relief from worries. Rise in society.

Happy - Something unpleasant to happen.

Hares - *To see* – Faithful friends.
- *Being chased by dogs* – Will escape from enemies.

Harlot - Will have jealous wife.

Harmony - Long and happy life.

Harp - *To see* – Death in the family. Slander.
- *Hear it* – Sadness.
- *Broken* – Illness
- *Playing it* – Be careful in all matters.

Harvest - *For farmer* – Prosperity.
- *For businessmen* – Lucrative bargains.

Hat - *Wearing new* – Change of place and success.
- *Lose* – Unsatisfactory outlook.
- *Taken off your head* – Enemies to injure you.

Hawk - Stiff business competition and rivalry.

Hate - A good friend in the time of need.

Hay - *Cut it* – Will have great influence in society.
- *Raking it* – Will be respected by gentry and nobility.

Head - *Bareheaded* – Worries.
- *Oiling* – Losses.
- *Of school* – Unfavourable change.
- *Of dead* – Worries.

Heart - *To see* – Sickness and failure.
- *Your diseased* – Too much blood in your system.
- *Yours palpitating* – Great trouble.
- *Suffocating* – Trouble in business.
- *Of animal* – Overcome your enemies.
- *To eat the heart* – Success in strange desires.

Heat - Anger and scolding in store for you.

Heaven - *To see* – gain of health, wealth, peace and spirituality.
- *To be in* – Promotion.

Hedge - You have to work hard for success.

Hedgehog - Will meet a friend after a long period.

Height - *Fall from* – Reversal in rank.
- *Climb to* – Respect and promotion.

Heir - Poverty.

Hell - Going to Pious nature.
- *Coming out* – Good deeds.

Hen - *To see* – Do not tell your secrets to others.
- *Hear crackle* – Joy, love and profit.
- *Lay eggs* – Gain.
- *With chicken* – Loss and damage.

Herbs - *Fragrant* – Good omen.
- *Poisonous* – Danger.
- *Sage* – Honour and advancement.
- *Thyme* – Happy marriage.
- *Balm* – Sickness and sure recovery.
- *Hore hound* – Chronic and incurable disease.
- *Warm wood* – Trials and trauma.

Heron - Loyalty may be expected from your beloved.

Hill - *To see* – Financial gains and social success.
- *Climbing to* – Hardwork rewarded.
- *Going down* – Loss, worries.

Hippopotamus - An exciting time is ahead.

Hit - Gain of beautiful woman.

Hockey - Will have busy time.

Hoe - *For man* – Will enjoy good health.
- *For young woman* – Lover will be an agriculturist.
- *To use* – Success.

Hogs - Pigs denote mixture of good and bad luck.

Holiday - Keep away from petty quarrels. Prosperous time.

Home - Depart from home. Prosperity and conjugal happiness.

Homicide - Committing homicide portends misfortune.

Honey - Eating honey signifies health, wealth and longlife.

Honeybees - Fortune.

Honeycomb - Success through hard work.

Honeymoon - Travels.

Hops - Wealth and receive legacy.

Horn - *Hear* – Receive intelligence from a friend.

Horns - *On your head* – Gain.

Horse - *To see* – Association with magic and divination.
- *To ride* – Sexual implications.
- *Fall from* – Worries. Reversal.
- *Black* – A good rank. Tendency to deception.
- *Red* – Good news.
- *White* – Prosperity.
- *Runaway* – Be careful of misuse of money.

Horseshoe - *To see* – Good fortune.
- *To find* – Success in lottery.

Hospital - Business prosperity. Happiness.

Hotel - *To see* – Shattering of hopes.
- *Luxuriant* – Sickness.
- *Flowers in* – Lustfulness.
- *Living in* – Desire for lucrative life.
- *Being manager* – Desire for power.

Hounds - Unproductive tasks.

House - *To see* – self-esteem.
- *Bedroom* – Inner reality.
- *Bathroom* – Clean your surroundings.
- *Dining room* – You will indulge in rituals.

- *Doors* – Movement in life.
- *Fence* – Intact/broken security.
- *Garden* – Growing/withering desires.
- *Kitchen* – Nourishment required.
- *Roof/ceiling* – Security required.
- *Stairs* – Ascend/descend in life.
- *Walls* – Limitation in working life.
- *Windows* – Will be able to see events unfolding.
- *Self Sitting in* – Happy news.
- *Climbing big house* – Gain. Promotion.
- *Jumping from* – Escape from evil.
- *Construction* – Fulfilment of wishes.
- *Disagreeable* – Frustrating family life.
- *Falling apart* – Finances need monitoring.
- *Double story* – Respect and honour.
- *Row of* – Happy domestic life.

Humming-birds - Travel to foreign country for business.

Hunger - *Feeling of* – Riches.

Hunting - Gain of object. Promotion.

Hurricane - Quarrels in the home.

Hurt - Projects will Succeed.

Husband - Your beloved is true to you.

Husbandry - *Plough* – Success and good marriage.
- *Yoke* – Unfavourable.
- *Scythe* – Injury from enemies. Disappointment in love.
- *Team* – Death in family.

Hymns - Death of a friend.

Ice - *To see* – Ambitions materialize in an expected way.
- *Floating* – Beware of jealous associates.
- *Walking on* – Distressing interferences.
- *For sailor* – Disaster.
- *For farmer* – Devastation of crops.

	- *For trader* – Unsuccessful speculation.
Icicles	- *For man* – Gook luck.
	- *For young woman* – Marriage with man of wealth.
Idiot	- *Yourself* – Competency for future engagement.
	- *Others* – Will receive favour from them.
Idle	- By perseverence you can gain anything.
Idol	- Expect a gift.
Ill	- Danger of falling into a temptation.
Illness	- To dream of being ill is a lucky sign.
Illumination	- Joyful occasion at hand.
Image	- Affection of children.
Imprison-ment	- An unexpected event is foretold.
Inability to escape	- Getting tied down in job, relationship.
Income	- Will be able to save money.
Indepen-dence	- Affair will go on as usual.
Industry	- Will rise above the common level.
Infirm	- *Yourself* – Health for yourself and children.
	- *Others* – Affliction.
Influence	- Obstacles will be encountered.
Inheritance	- Loss of money.
Injury	- *To yourself* – Take care of everything.
	- *Inflicting to others* – Realisation of wishes thwarted.
Ink	- Unexpected but welcome news.
Inn	- Poverty and want of success in undertakings.
Insane	- Domestic happiness and social enjoyment.
Insanity	- Take care of rampant jealousy.
Insect	- Should work hard for success.
Insolvent	- Increased trade and good return.

Insult - You will receive an honour.

Intemperance - *Intemperate in eating* – Sickness.
- *Intemperate in drinking* – Troubles.

Intoxicated - *Self* – Warning of troubles ahead.

Introduction - New friends will be made.

Invalid - Minor worries that will soon pass.

Invitation - Control your temper to avoid an estrangement.

Invite - *Being invited* – Troubles.
- *You invite* – Success.

Iron - *To see* – Success through new friends. Rise in position.
- *Hurt with* – Will receive damage.
- *Trade in* – Losses and misfortune.

Island - *To see* – Happiness and comfort.
- *Running to* – Desire to escape from the present.
- *Many people on* – Desire to have new friends.

Itch - Troubles in business and love.

Ivory - *To see* – Faith and loyalty in your married life.
- *Huge pieces* – Financial success.

Ivy - *Growing on trees* – Adherence by lover, husband/ wife, friend.
- *Clinging to walls* – Clandestine meetings.

Jackal - *Howling of* – Death.

Jackdaw - *Crosses your path* – Bitter enemies will injure you.
- *You catch it* – Enemies will not succeed.

Jaggery - Poverty.

Jail - *To see* – Small worries.
- *Be in* – Freedom from embarrassment.
- *Escape from* – Favourable change in circumstances.

Jailer - *Alone* – Desire to elude responsibilities.
- *With people* – Desire for taking revenge.

Jam - A pleasant surprise.

Jar - *Full* – Good for business.

- *Empty* – Efforts will be in vain.

Jaundice
- *You have* – Sickness. Poverty. Disagreement.
- *Wife/husband has* – Doubtful fidelity.

Jealousy - Troubles. Anxiety.

Jew - Business prosperity.

Jeweller - A small loss should be expected.

Jewellery
- *To see* – High ambitions.
- *Broken* – Disappointments.
- *Tarnished* – Business problems.
- *Cankered* – Friends will ditch.
- *Expensive* – Lack of good things.
- *Wearing* – Happiness.
- *Buying* – Rise in status.
- *Receiving* – Rise in fortune.
- *Received as gift* – Happy wedded life.
- *Lose* – Take special care of personal property.
- *Store* – Desire to display.

Jewels
- *To see* – Prosperity.
- *Lover gives* – He will marry you.

Job
- *Searching* – Disturbed mind.
- *Getting* – New opportunities for success.
- *Losing* – Misfortune.

Jockey - Beware of speculative activities.

Jocking - Accusation. Disrespect.

Jolly - *With person* – He will contribute to your mirth.

Journey
- *Yourself on* – Profits.
- *Road* – Exciting time.
- *Rail* – Quarrels and gain of money.
- *Air* – Difficulties and losses.
- *Sad departure* – Meetings will be after long time.
- *Long distance* – Accomplishment.
- *Accident* – Disagreeable event will unfold.
- *Friend on* – Harmonious companions.

Judge - *To see* – Your worries will soon pass.
- *You are* – A good position.
- *Standing before* – cofusion.
- *Convicts you* – Good fortune.
- *Aquits you* – Unsuccessful adventure.

Jug - *Drink out of* – Journey.
- *Good liquid in* – Pleasent journey.
- *Avoidable liquid in* – Sorrow and trouble.
- *Long* – Long journey.
- *Short* – Short journey.

Jumper - Favourable for those in love.

Jumping - It tempted, do not fall.

Jungle - *To see* – Do as you yourself think right.
- *Walking through* – Escape from troubles.
- *Wet* – Happiness.
- *Red* – Worries.

Juniper - *To see* – Unlucky. Sickness will prolong.
- *Gathering berries* – Prosperity and Joy.

Jury - Success through friends.

Kennel - Your friends are faithful.

Kernel - Will be wealthy through a legacy.

Kettle - Peace, prosperity, happiness and hope.

Keys - *To see* – Foretells a change and riches.
- *To find* – Lucky omen.
- *To lose* – Unpleasant adventure.
- *To give* – A marriage.
- *To receive* – Disappointness and displeasure.
- *Unlocking* – problems will be understood and solved.
- *Locking* – Successful selection of partner.
- *Broken* – Pertends separation.

Kill - *An animal* – Desire to get rid of a difficult situation.

Killing - *Being killed* – Good news, Long life.
- *Some body* – Will help others.

- *Defenceless person* – Predicts sorrow and failures.
- *In self-defence* – Promotion.
- *A friend* – Good health.
- *A parent* – Catastrophe.
- *An enemy* – Warning of trouble.
- *A businessman* – Security.
- *A beast* – Victory over enemy.
- *A bird or bee* – Loss in business.
- *A serpent* – Separation.
- *And eating an animal* – Profit in business.

King - *To see* – An introduction. A gift. Honour or promotion.
- *Being* – Desire to rule others.

Kiss - *To see* – New Friends.
- *Being kissed* – Faithful lover.
- *Kissed by lover* – True lover.
- *Kissing stranger* – False friends.
- *Kissing life partner* – Unfaithful companion.

Kitchen - New household things will be yours.

Kite - *To see* – A welcome letter is on the way.
- *Making* – Not to speculate.
- *Fly* – Desire to be an extrovert.
- *Flying high* – Elevation in life. Promotion.
- *Flying it* – Fortune.
- *Blows away* – Very bad omen.

Kitten - Beware of a "certain" friend. Happiness.

Knee - Hindrances, troubles, grief.

Knife - Poverty, enemies and evil designs.

Knitting - Do not make or listen to gossip.

Knives - Quarrels. Anxious times.

Knots - *To see* – Minor worries.
- *Tie one* – Time is needed to be free.

Krishna - Spiritual evolvement.

Labour - *To see* – Wealth.

- *Yourself* – Easy passage through life.
- *Men toiling* – Profitable work and health.
- *Animals labouring* – Prosperity.

Lace - Happiness to follow.

Ladder - *To see* – Success through your own efforts.
- *Ascending* – Wealth. Bright prospects.
- *Reach top* – Honour and glory.
- *Not reaching the top* – Unable to adjust to success.
- *Fall from* – Disaster.
- *Broken* – Threatens failure.

Lady - *Talk to* – Gain of wealth.
- *Kiss her* – Meeting with beloved.
- *See her hairs* – Defeat in law suit.

Lake - *To see* – Romance, pleasure.
- *Of clear water* – Honour and money.
- *Of muddy water* – Trouble. Insolvencies.
- *Storm* – Conflicts.
- *Surrounded by verdure* – Desire to release an urge.
- *Barren surroundings* – Financial crisis.
- *Overturned boat in* – Confusion.

Lamb - *To see* – Joy for dreamer.
- *Dead* – Unfortunate news.
- *Lost* – Uncertainty and struggle.

Lame - Difficulties and disappointment.

Lament - Rejoicing over property and conduct of children.

Lamp - *To see* – Respect and gain.
- *Lighting* – Long life.
- *Extinguishes* – Short life.
- *Burning bright* – Success in profession.
- *Carrying dim one* – Unhappiness. Sickness.
- *Row of* – Party or wedding.

Land - *To See* – Wealth and happiness.
- *To level* – Gain of object.

- *To possess* – Wealth and independance.
- *To buy* – Change of residence.
- *To sell* – Adverse circumstances.

Lane - *Moving in a narrow one* – Difficulties.

Lantern - *Carrying it* – Wishes will be fulfilled.
- *Stumble while carrying it* – Trouble.

Lark - Health and prosperity.

Laughing - *Self* – Forebodes tears.
- *Children* – Happy time ahead.

Laughter - Expect tears which will be healed by time.

Laundry - Trifling problems should not be ignored.

Laurel - *To receive* – Pleasure and prosperity.
- *By woman* – Birth of child.
- *To young* – Speedy marriage.

Lawn - *Like carpet* – Realization of ambition.
- *Crushing it* – Hindrances in plans.
- *For lovers* – Happy union.

Law Suit - Difficulties.

Lawyer - Difficulties are encroaching.

Lead - Troubles and quarrels.

Leap - Business, success or promotion.

Learning - Will attain respect by your diligence.

Leasing - House or building foretells business improvement.

Leather - Business will be dull and slow.

Leaves - *Green* – Prosperity.
- *Withered/Brown* – Worries. Bad crops.

Leave-taking - Serious illness.

Lecture - *Lecturing/Listening* – Important decision to be made.

Ledger - Beware of your subordinates and servants.

Leech - Sickness or injury.

Legs - *To see* – Failure. Loss. Ill-health.
- *Well shaped* – Loss of judgement.
- *Wounded* – Losses and fever.
- *Wooden* – Will demean yourself.
- *Have three or more* – More avenues.

Lemons - *To see* – Even a pleasant marriage will be troubling.
- *To eat* – will be attacked by a dangerous disease.

Lending - Losses and poverty.

Leopard - Foreign travel, full of difficulties.

Leprosy - Sorrow, disgrace and probably imprisonment.

Letters - *To see* – beware of extravagance. Disagreements.
- *Anonymous* – Troubled mind.
- *Bringing bad news* – Ill-health.
- *To send* – Will be doing a generous act.
- *To receive* – Unexpected news or gift.
- *To read* – Good news.

Lettuce - Troubles and difficulties.

Library - Success through well-known person.

Lice - Difficulties in profession.

Life-boat - *To see* – Easy life.
- *Saved by* – Success in your affairs.

Light-house - Will commit some blunder in judgement.

Lighting - Your love is true to you.

Lightning - *To see* – Desire to thrust love upon someone.
- *With rain or storm* – Unlucky.
- *Striking someone* – Danger.
- *For farmer* – Good crop.
- *For sailor* – Good voyage.

Lights - *To see* – Gain of knowledge.
- *Bright or torches* – Success. Riches. Honour.
- *Personally carrying* – Help from friends.
- *Others carrying* – Loss to enemies.

	- *Off and on* – Danger will be averted.
	- *Carrying to office* – Fame, publicity.
	- *Flickering* – Ill-health warning.
	- *Extinguishes in prayer room* – Death of someone.
	- *Not able to light* – Evil to children.
Lily	- Happiness and prosperity.
Linen	- *Clean white* – Domestic felicity. Business success.
	- Dirty – Sickness and wretchedness.
Lion	- *To see* – Exciting times, adventure, and romance.
	- *Young* – New enterprises.
	- *To ride* – Favour from seniors and government.
	- *Subdue a lion* – Victory.
	- *Attacked by* – Enemy succeeds.
	- *Overpowered by* – Enemy wins.
	- *Caged* – Abilities will manifest.
	- *Controlling* – Success in business.
	- *To hear roar of* – Sudden advancement.
	- *Head* – Fall from power.
	- *Skin* – Happiness.
Lips	- *Lovely* – Affluence and harmony.
	- *Red and lusty* – Good health.
	- *Ugly* – Wrong decisions.
	- *Dry and chapped* – Sickness.
	- *Swollen* – Unhealthy desires.
	- *Thin* – Knowledge of intricate subjects.
Liquors	- *Drink brandy* – Will reside in foreign land.
	- *Drink rum* – Partnership in shipping circle.
	- *Drink gin* – Will live in populous town in poverty.
	- *Drink whisky* – Will have reversal in circumstances.
Litigation	- Business reversal.
Lizard	- Misfortune, secret enemies, sudden gain of wealth.
Load	- *Carrying a heavy one* – Struggles for survival.
	- *Able to carry* – Will overcome troubles.

Loan - Beware of deceit. A trick might be played on you.

Loaves - Dearth of resources.

Lock - *To see* – Perplexity, confusion.
- *On trunk* – Thwarted ambitions.
- *On door* – Desire for new openings.
- *With key* – Happy love affair, business success.
- *Without key* – Failures.
- *To close* – Worries.
- *To open* – Happiness.

Locomotive - Travel, or arrival of a dear friend.

Looking glass - Prosperity to ensue. Discard overconfidence.

Lost - *Self* – Frustrations, losses, disappointments.
- *Something* – Desire will be granted.

Lottery - *Ticket* – Anxiety. Stress.
- *Winning* – Treacherous friends seeking your ruin.
- *Loses* – Money will be earned.

Louse (Lice) - Poor health and strong enemies.

Love - *Of family* – Great happiness.
- *Of parents* – Fortune and elevation.
- *Of friends* – Business Success.
- *Of animals* – Foretells contentment.
- *Be loved* – Faithful friends. Prosperity.
- *Of beloved* – Victory of enemies.
- *For a woman* – Safe delivery of a child.
- *Fails* – Will be despodent.
- *Success* – Contentment and freedom from anxiety.
- *Emotional* – Satisfaction in your working.

Love letter - *Writing* – Happiness.
- *Reading* – Some good news.
- *Receiving* – Fortune.

Lovely - *Yourself* – Expect sickness.

- *Others* – Will marry cheerful and handsome/beautiful spouse.

Lover - *Yours* – A happy married life.

Lovers - *Others* – Wishes will be fulfilled.

Loving - *Someone* – Satisfaction with present happenings.
- *Unwanted* – Possible heart trouble.
- *Animals* – Contentment and fortune.
- *Children* – Happiness.
- *Wife* – Luck and prosperity.
- *Husband* – Be careful with rivals.
- *Friend* – May receive bad news about the friend.
- *Relatives* – Financial loss.
- *Being loved* – Loss of false promise.

Luck - Disappointments.

Luggage - A worrying time is ahead.

Lute - *Playing it* – Envious person will harm you.

Luxury - Poverty. Troubles.

Lying - Not a good omen.

Lynx - Enemies to injure you.

Lyre - *Listen to* – Pleasure.
- *Playing on* – Undivided affection of a man.

Machine gun - Sexual impulses.

Machinery - Entanglement in love,business involvement.

Mad dog - Success will crown your efforts.

Madness - Vigour of intellect, tide of prosperity.

Magic - Desire to display talent, change for better.
- *Performer* – Higher learning.

Magical - *Success* – Pleasant surprises.
- *Practice* – Profitable changes.
- *Sorcery* – Upheavels.
- *Effect* – Visions.

Magistrate - *Convicts you* – Bad days ahead.
- *Acquits you* – Good days ahead.

Magnet - *To see* – Snares will be laid on your path.
- *To use* – Plans for selfish purpose.

Magpie - Early marriage and then loss of your partner.

Maid - Marriage or union.

Malice - Someone bears you malice signifies progress by marriage.

Malt - *To see* – Prosperity and comfortable old age.
- *To brew it to beer* – Marriage.

Man - *Young* – Sexual desires.
- *Old* – Journey.
- *Laughing* – Quarrels. Disappointment.
- *Weeping* – Good news.
- *Blind* – Will help friends.
- *Mental* – Worries.

Mansion - Longing for higher plane of living.

Man-slaughter - Robbery, fire, destruction of property.

Map - Urge to fulfil certain desires.

Marigolds - Happy marriage. Promotion. Honour.

Mariner - News from abroad. Seafaring transactions.

Market - Domestic enjoyment. Good trade.

Marmalade - *Eating alone* – Sickness.
- *Eating with others* – Kind friends and cheer.

Marriage - *Own* – Unpleasant news. Danger. Grief.
- *To see* – Happiness.
- *Re-marrying* – Distruct. Deep-seated jealousy.
- *Bigamy* – Suspicion of some relative.
- *With old lady* – Unexpected wealth.
- *Assisting* – Advancement.
- *Attending* – Difficulties.

Mars - Quarrels, robbery, theft.

Marsh - *Get along* – Sorrows and difficulties.
- *Get out of* – Remaining life will be manageable.

Mask - *To see* – Unreliable persons around.
- *Yourself wearing* – Desire to withhold past actions.
- *Others wearing* – Will be victim of deception.
- *Many wearing* – Envious friends and associates.

Master - *To see* – Business changes or rise in your work.
- *Yourself* – Losses and unhappiness.

Mat - *Being stolen* – Robbery or theft foretold.

Match - Be guided by reason and common sense.

Meadow - Peace and happiness in the near future.

Meal - New understanding. Busy life.

Measles - Riches are about to drop into your lap.

Meat - *To eat* – Good time.

Medal - You, or someone near to you, will receive honours.

Medals - Loss of character and depravity.

Medicine - *To take* – Good health, environment.
- *To give* – You will hurt a reliable person.
- *Pleasant* – Trouble followed by gain.
- *Unpalatable* – Deep sorrow or loss.

Melancholy - A gratifying news.

Melons - Marriage with rich foreigner, and live in foreign land.

Mendicant - *Be a beggar* – will amass wealth.
- *Accosted by beggar* – Troubles through false friend.

Mermaid - Beware of a friend of the opposite sex.

Merry - Sadness and sickness.

Message - *To receive* – Changes.
- *To send* – Unpleasant situations.

Metal - Monetary benefits.

Mice - *To see* – Insincerity and deception.

- *To kill* – Victory over enemies.
- *Escapes* – Domestic troubles, unreliable loyalty.

Microscope - Failures and losses.

Midget
- *To see* – Desire to hurt close friend.
- *Being one* – Feeling of helplessness.

Milk
- *See it* – Success.
- *Drink it* – Joy.
- *Spilling* – Loss of money.
- *Sour* – Domestic problems.
- *Hot* – Make efforts to accumulate money.
- *Selling* – Bad trade and disappointments in love.
- *Give* – Prosperity and happy marriage.
- *Milking a cow* – Healthy cattle. Good crops.

Milkman - Opportunities will soon be knocking at your door.

Mill - Your dearest wish will come true.

Mine - Beware of jealousy and falsehoods.

Minister
- *To see* – Honour and promotion.
- *To hear* – Evil designs for you.
- *Taking oath* – Official punishment and displeasure.
- *Yourself* – Will usurp other's rights.

Minuet (a slow dance)
- *To see dancing* – Happiness.
- *To hear* – Congenial companions
- *To be* – Fortune.

Mire - *Wading in* – Toil and trouble.

Mirror
- *To see* – Prosperity to come. Fall in love.
- *Broken or hazy* – Difficulties and tribulations.

Miser - Troubles and poverty.

Miserable - Unexpected good fortune.

Misfortune - Success in business. A good life partner.

Missing
- *Train/Aeroplane* – Get ready for events.
- *Station* – Missed opportunity.
- *Things* – Loss of confidence and direction.

Mist - Useful plans for advancement.

Mole - Good health.

Monastery - Change of place or occupation.

Money - *To see* – Prosperity. Happiness in love.
- *Getting* – Power will be acquired.
- *Gain of* – Happiness.
- *To find* – Sudden advancement.
- *To give* – Expenses.
- *Paying* - Prosperity.
- *To receive* – Good fortune. Birth of a child.
- *To Count* – Many children.
- *Loan of* – Loss.
- *Losing* – Gloomy affairs.
- *To steal* – Do not drive sharp bargains.
- *To waste* – Advice to other. Fear of loss.
- *Looking at* – Prosperity.
- *Stacking* – Happiness.
- *Spending* – Failure through unwise deal.

Monk - *To see* – Family upheavels.
- *Yourself* – Loss and disease.

Monkey - *To see* – Mischief from a good friend, worries.
- *To feed* – Betrayals.
- *Dead* – Enemies will fade.

Moon - *To see* – Birth of son, fame, love affair.
- *Waxing* – Growth of imagination.
- *Waning* – Loss of health.
- *New* – Good fortune.
- *Full* – Over-sentimentality.
- *Light in house* – Gain of money.
- *Red* – Troubles beyond one's control.
- *Cloudy* – Worries.
- *Eclipsed* – Disease.

Mortage - *Taking* – Lack of good economy.

- *To hold* – Wish for great wealth and prosperity.

Mortician - *For stranger* – Anxiety over perplexing difficulty.
- For relative – Differences will be sorted out.

Mortury - Unhappiness followed by rejoicing.

Mosquito - Troubles through enemies.

Moss - *To see* – Subordinate positions and placements.
- *Grows* – Top positions and honour.

Moth - *To see* – Worries and quarrels.

Mother - *Yours* – Successful enterprises.
- *Talk to* – Good news.
- *Calling her* – Guilty conscience, sorrow.
- *A call from* – Warning for improved action.
- *A cry from* – Troubles around.
- *Dead* – Intolerance.
- *To be one* – Sadness.

Mother-in-law - Wife is annoyed.

Moths - Enemies to undermine your position. Separation from loved.

Motor car - Financial prosperity. You receive a gift.

Mountain - *Climbing* – Difficulties ahead; progress in profession.
- *Descending* – Change in affairs.

Mourning - Health and wealth.

Mouse - Friends to harm you.

Movies - Desire to get away from monotony.

Murder - *To see* – Danger averted.
- *To commit* – Brook no interference.
- *Of yourself* – Desire to overcome hardship.

Muscle - *Yours well developed* – Encounter with enemies and success.
- *Yours shrunken* – Failures.

Muscle Man - Good health.

Museum - *To see* – Take advice for your problems.
- *Unattractive* – Disputes and displeasure.

Mushrooms - *To see* – Losing law suits and unhealthy desires.
- *To eat* – Humiliation.
- *To gather* – Gradual riches.

Music - *Hear* – Grab any opportunity that comes your way.
- *Pleasing* – Augurs prosperity.
- *Depressing* – Creative forces will go wasted.
- *Discordant* – Domestic or emotional uncertainty.

Musical Instrument - *To see* – Pleasure.
Broken – Disturbed mind.

Musician - A gay time is ahead.

Musk - Joy and agreeable affairs.

Mystery - *Bewilderment* – Strangers will burden you. Failure.
- *Studying* – Research career, learning and fortune.

Nails - *To see* – Difficulties in business.
- *To cut* – Get rid of difficulties.

Naked - *Himself* – Embracement, scandal, disgrace.
- *Herself* – Unhappiness.
- *Others* – Will yield to immoral temptation.
- *A woman* – High ambition.
- *A beautiful woman* – Good earnings.
- *An ugly woman* – Dissatisfation of desires.
- *Wife* – Ill fame.
- *Sleeping with woman* – Hatred of someone towards you.
- *Sleeping with man* – Confusion.
- *Walking* – Betrayal by friends.

Nakedness - Loss of friends, but you may fall in love.

Navy - *You are in* – Desires to avoid present encumbrances.
- *You are happy in* – Business or marital difficulties.

Neck - Take care of your health.

Necklace - *To see* – Prosperous time and wedding envisaged.
- *To receive* – Marriage.
- *To lose* Sorrow.

Need - Wealth and favour will arrive soon.

Needle - *To see* – Domestic or other worries.
- *To use* – Loss of sympathy.
- *Threading it* – Patience is desired.
- *To look for* – Useless worries.
- *Finding one* – New friends.
- *Breaking it* – Desire for seclusion.
- *Sewing with* – Need of good friends.

Negress/ Negro - A sign of good luck, be careful of confiding in people.

Neighbour - Quarrels and bickerings.

Nervous - Will be valient in future conflicts.

Nest - *To see* – Desires will be fulfilled.
- *Having broken eggs* – Failure and distress.

Nets - *Catching something* – Binding contract or deal.
- *Torn* – Loss of money, employment or property.
- *You are caught in* – Wish to avoid entanglement.

Nettle - *To see* – Health and wealth.
- *Stinge by* – Vexation and disappointment.

News - *A strange news* – Serious trouble for loved ones.

Newspaper - *To see* – Exposure of your frauds.
- *Reading it* – Reputation in danger.
- *Printing it* – Will make new friends.
- *Failing to read* – Failures.

Newspaper Reporter - *To see unwillingly* – Irritation and anger.
Yourself – Journeys and gains.

New year - *Happiness* – Prosperity.
- *Sadness* – Portends inauspicious connections.

Night - *Walking on a dark night* – Losses and misfortune.

- *Overtaken by night* – Competency to adversity.

Nightingale - Harbinger of joy, success and prosperity.

Nightmare - Foolish and imprudent habit.

Nine pins - Playing at this game foretells business reverses.

Nobility - Trouble is about to visit.

Noise - *Hear* – Expect interference in your plans and wishes.

Noodles - *To see* – Abnormal appetite and desires.

Nose - *To see yours* – Achieve the targets.
- *Shrunk* – Failures.
- *Bleeding* – Disaster. Expensive law suit.
- *Hairy* – Free will to work.

Nudity - Desire for openness and transparency. Vulnerability.

Numbers - Financial fortune.

Nun - Marriage in the family. Spiritual thought.

Nupitals - *To see* – Will safeguard your interests.
- *Yourself* – Death.
- *Assist at* – Advancement in life.

Nurse - *To see* – Good health and happiness.
- *Yourself* – Many friends.

Nursing - *A baby* – Desire for parenthood. Promotion.
- *Sick* – Fame.

Nutmegs - *To see* – Prosperity. Journeys.

Nuts - *To see* – Do not trust people blindly. Be secretive.
- *Eating* – Wishes will be granted.
- *Gathering* – Happy love life.
- *Having good kernel* – Will be wealthy by legacy.

Oak - *Tree* – Increased income, advancement.
- *Full of acorns* – Unbounded prosperity.
- *Withered* – Poverty and loss.
- *Forest* – Prosperity.
- *Blasted* – Sudden and shocking surprises.

Oar - *Rowing a boat* – Disappointments from services rendered.
- *Lose one* – Useless efforts to please others.
- *Broken* – Interruption in anticipated plan.

Oatmeal - *Cooking it* – Wish to rule others.
- *To eat* – Pleasant times.

Oats - *To see* – Bountiful harvest. Flourishing business.
- *Horse eating it* – Projects will be completed.

Ocean - *To see* – Desire to be reborn.
- *On shipboard* – Desire to travel far away.
- *Calm* – Good fortune.
- *In storm* – Disturbances, enmity.

Odour - *Sweet* – Beautiful woman to co-operate.
- *Disgusting* – Unreliable servants.

Offence - *Being charged of* – Altercation and desire of revenge.

Office - *To see* – A change in business or professional life.
- *Working in* – Money matters need attention.
- *Hold one* – High aspiration.
- *Turned out of* – Death and loss of property.

Oil - *To massage* – Shame for men, good for women.
- *To drink* – Beginning of new job.

Old people - A sign of long life.

Olive - *Gathering* – Peace, delight.
- *Eating* – Rise above present position.

Onions - *To see* – Expect a legacy or at least a gift.
- *To cut or peel* – Domestic quarrels. Hard work.
- *To eat* – Gains. Treasure.
- *Growing in field* – Opposition to plans.

Opera - *Attend one* – Augment business holdings.

Operation - Recovery from illness.

Opulence - Will be poor for long time.

Oranges - *To see* – Carefree time, wedding.

- *On tree* – Good health.
- *Girl eating* – May forefeit love of fiance. Family jars.
- *Man eating* – Unexpected complications in career.

Orator - *Under spell of* – Will help unworthy.
- *Fall in love with* – Fall prey to show business.

Orchard - *To see* – You will make new friends.
- *Of blossoming trees* – Fulfilment of love.
- *Of ripe fruits* – Happy home, ample income.
- *Gathering fruits* – Will be heir to some property.
- *Unproductive* – Rough road to achievement.

Orchestra - *To hear* – Popularity.
- *Playing in* – Advancement in your occupation.

Organ - *To see* – A good sign for those in love.
- *Playing it* – Social honour and awards.
- *To hear it* – Many friends.
- *In church* – Warning of separation.

Ornaments - A lean financial period is ahead.

Orphans - *To see* – Profits through a stranger.
- *Female* – Wife will be rich.

Ostrich - An unexpected present or news from abroad.

Oven - *Baking* – Moderate success in trade.
- *Burn bread in* – Disaster.
- *Red hot* – Love from family and friends.
- *Broken* – Trouble from children and servents.

Overboard - *Fallen overboard at sea* – Poverty, sickness.

Overcoat - *To see* – Contradictions.
- *Wear a new* – Unexpected honour.
- *Lose your* – Avoid speculations.
- *To borrow* – Misfortune through mistakes of others.

Owl - *To see* – Be careful in all matters. Defamation.
- *To hear* – Ill-health of close ones.
- *To see dead* – Escape from disease.

Ox - *To see* – Strength will surface.

	- *Healthy* – You will lead your community.
	- *Fat* – You will rise beyond your expectations.
	- *Lean* – Fortune to dwindle.
	- *Dead* – Bereavement.
	- *Grazing* – Accumulation of immense wealth.
	- *Drinking* – You will possess an estate or a beloved.
Oysters	- *To see* – Many children.
	- *To eat* – Strong desire to get money and status.
	- *To deal in* – Win a sweetheart or fortune.
	- *Gathering shells* – Fleeting pleasure.
Oyster shells	- *To see* – Frustrated efforts.
Pacify	- *For men* – Will be labouring for the advancement of others.
	- *For woman* – Devoted husband or friends.
Packet	- *Coming in* – Pleasant time ahead.
	- *Going out* – Losses and disappointment.
Packing	- *Luggage* – Repressed desire of travel.
	- *Not complete* – Frustrations of daily life.
Page	- *To see* – Undesirable romantic impulses.
Pagoda	- *To see* – A longing desire to travel in oriental places.
	- *Yourself in* – Desire for sexual union.
Pail	- Troubles in the near future.
Pain	- Unexpected gain.
Paint	- *Appreciate* – Good luck in business.
	- *Your house* – Sickness in the family.
Painting	- *To see* – To express ambition.
	- *Of beautiful landscapes* – Poverty and bad luck.
	- *Of white house* – Funeral.
Palace	- A happy event in the near future.
Pall	- Prepare for wedding.
Palsy	- Uneasiness of mind.

Pancakes - Fruition of hope. Joyous occasion.

Panther - *To see* – Disappointment, cancellation of contract.
- *To overpower* – Joy.
- *To kill* – Wealth and position after a long struggle.
- *To run away from* – Disgrace.
- *Frightens you* – Disappointment.
- *Hear its voice* – Unfavourable news.

Pantomime - Beware of deceitful persons.

Paper - Financial gift or success.

Parade - Make a decision after careful scrutiny.

Paradise - *To be in* – Loyal friends.
- *For mothers* – Obedient children.
- *For lovers* – Promises faithfulness.
- *For sick* – Speedy recovery.
- *Lost on way to* – Dwindling fortunes.

Paralysis - *Experiencing* – Anxiety, fear and indecision.

Parasol - Worries will overwhelm you.

Parcel - *To see* – May receive a gift.
- *Being delivered to you* – Surprising return of absentees.
- *Carry it* – To perform unpleasant task.
- *Drop it* – Failure of a deal.

Parchment - Will be accused of crimes from which you will be acquitted.

Parents - *To see* – Happy times are ahead.
- *In your home* – Pleasant changes.
- *Looking cheerful* – Harmony all around.
- *Looking robust* – Business and love to flourish.
- *Looking dull* – Disappointments.
- *Looking sickly* – Fruitless effort.
- *After their death* – Approaching difficulties.

Park - Faithful lover and speedy marriage.

Parliament - *To see proceedings* – War as well as peace.

Parrot - Do not confide in pretending friends. Journey.

Parting - Disappointment and jealousy.

Partner - *Life* – Disharmony.
- *Business* – Losses.

Partridge - *To see* – Misfortune.
- *Fly away* – Will overcome difficulties.

Party - *To see* – A good time is coming.
- *Attending* – Honour.
- *Throwing* – Respect and position.
- *Mad and wild* – Unwise selection of friends.

Passenger - *Yourself* – Reflects dissatisfaction.
- *Greet them* – Your lot will improve.
- *Others leaving you behind* – Lost opportunity.

Passing bell - Bereavement of a relative.

Passion - Sincere and true friends.

Pastry - *To see* – Likely to be deceived
- *To eat* – Good friends.
- *Cooking it* – Failure of misintended efforts.

Patch - *On your clothes* – No false ego. Riches.
- *On others' clothes* – Approaching misery.
- *For a woman* – Troubles against happiness.
- *Woman hiding it* – Should be discreetly secretive.
- *Family patching* – Scarcity of means.

Patent - *To see* – Disease.
- *To secure* – Carefulness.
- *Fail to secure* – Failure.
- *Buy it* – Unwaranted journey.

Path - *Good* – Success in trade, love, farming.
- *Crooked and thorny* – Treacherous friends.

Patterns - This is time to buy new things.

Paunch - *To see* – Wealth without oppulence.

- *Shrivelled* – Reverses.

Pauper - Gain and riches.

Pawnbroker - Trial, law suits and unbearable losses.

Peaches - *To see* – Happiness, peace, prosperity.
- *Eating* – Wealth or love.
- *On tree* – Work will be rewarded.

Peacock - *To see* – Mixed fortunes. Marriage with rich widow.
- *To hear* – Undulating thoughts.

Pearls - *To see* – Die as rich and great man.
- *Receive as gift* – Gala celebrations.
- *Lose or break a string* – Misunderstandings.

Pears - Ups and downs ahead.

Peas - *Eating* – Prosperity.
- *See growing* – Fortune, happy marriage.
- *To plant* – Hopes well grounded and to materialize.
- *To gather* – Fruitful plans.
- *Canned* – Dwindling and usurping future.
- *Dried* – Overtaking your health.
- *Eating dried* – After success a minor setback.

Pebbles - Petty jealousy or selfishness.

Pen - *To see* – Complications are ahead.
- *Refuses to write* – Will be charged for breach of morality.
- *Writes smoothly* – Expect a good news.

Pencil - You will receive an important letter.

Penny - *Counting* – Economical worries.
- *To lose* – Admonition to be economical.
- *To find* – Desire for more lucrative business.

Pension - *Programmed* – Will hear degrading expressions.
- *Drawing* – Friends to help.
- *Not able to draw* – Lose wealth and friends.

People - *Crowd of* – Quarrels in the family.

Pepper - Troubles in business.

Peram bulator - A child will be the focus of incidences.

Perfume - *To inhale* – Happiness.
- *To apply* – Will seek and gain adulation.
- *To receive* – Fascinating experiences.
- *To distil* – Happy environs and associates.
- *To spill* – Loss of favourite object.
- *To break container of* – Disaster.
- *Get suffocated by* – Fall in your mental abilities.

Perjury - Future imprudence. Contempt and neglect.

Phantom - Difficulties.

Pheasants - *To see* – Money is coming to you.
- *Flying across* – A legacy.
- *Flying away* – Law suit.

Photograph - Beware of jealousy and rivalry.

Physic - A passing unpleasantness.

Physician - *To see* – Good and bad time.
- *For men* – Gossiping.
- *For women* – Frivolous pastime.
- *For sick women* – Sickness and sorrow.

Piano - *To see* – Happy tidings. Beware of extravagance.
- *To play* – Difficulties to overcome.
- *To hear* – Harmony and health.
- *Pleasant music* – Winning friends.
- *Discordant notes* – Encounter difficulties.
- *Sad music* – Sorrowful events.
- *Broken* – Unsatisfactory results.
- *Old* – Be careful.

Pickpocket - *To see* – Loss due to enemity.
- *To pickpocket* – Displeasure.
- *Being picked* – Loss of regards.

Picnic - *Attending* – Foresight will lead you to success.
- *To observe* – Happiness.
- *Disturbance at* – Difficulties in business and personal affairs.

Pictures - *To see* – Deception by friends.
- *To make* – Unremunerative enterprise.
- *To destroy* – Success against heavy odds.
- *To buy* – Foretells worthless speculation.

Pier - *To see* – If unmarried, likely to meet your life partner.
- *To stand upon* – Honours.
- *Strive to reach* – Loss of distinction.

Pig - *To see* – Greed will overtake you. True affection.
- *Fat* – Reasonable success.
- *Wallowing* – Hurtful associates.

Pigeon - *See/hear* – Domestic harmony. Lucky for lovers.
- *Flying* – Freedom from misunderstanding. Knowledge.
- *Shoot at* – Warning against cruelty.

Pilgrim - *To see* – Long and misplaced journey.
- *Yourself* – Portends struggles with poverty.
- *Approaching you* – Deceit is foreshadowed.
- *Leaves you* – Thoughtfulness desired.

Pilgrimage - Auspicious omen.

Pill - *To take* – Responsibilities to befall.
- *To give* – Criticism awaited.

Pillow - Successful event.

Pilot - Desire to direct others.

Pimples - Will be admired.

Pine - Success. Happiness.

Pineapples - Happy settlement. An invitation to a feast.

Ping-pong - Desire for teamspirit.

Pipe - *To see* – Try to maintain peace or you will be

quarrelling.
- *Broken* – Poor health and poverty.
- *Smoking* – Temperamental differences with close ones.

Pirate
- *To see* – Suspicion of associates.
- *Yourself* – Unethical practices.
- *Caught by* – Foreign travel and riches.

Pistol
- *To see* – Bad fortune.
- *To own* – Displaying a low character.
- *To shoot* – Marriage with passionate and industrious person.
- *To hear* – Calamity. Someone to ruin your interest.

Pit
- *Descend* – Hazardous ventures.
- *Fall into* – Misfortune Losses.

Pitcher
- *To see* – Desire to make new friends.
- *Broken* – Loss of friends.

Plague
- *To see* – Poor returns in business.
- *Afflicted* – Successful manoeuvring for wealth.
- *Trying to escape* – Serious troubles.

Plank - Financially Difficult objectives.

Plants in pots - Exposure of secrets.

Platform - Unwanted admirers may cause you trouble.

Play
- *Watching* – Amusement and happiness.
- *Taking part* – Displeasure.

Pleasure - Disappointments and difficulties.

Plough - Steady gain and increase of trade.

Ploughing - Wealth through hard efforts.

Plow - Activity, which will be handled successfully.

Plums
- *To see* – Hurdles will be overcome.
- *Dried plums (prunes)* – Wait for auspicious time.
- *Gather green plums* – Sickness in the family.

Pocket - Be careful in all your deals.

Pocket book - *Finding one* – Desire to have more wealth.
- *Losing one* – Disappointments.
- *Empty* – Disagreements with best friends.
- *Filled with bills* – Good luck.

Poison - *Taking it* – Worries and grief.
- *To see* – Desire to eliminate an unwanted person.

Poker - *Playing* – Trusting luck in everyday life.
- *For self-defence* – unfair plot to damage your reputation.
- *To stir up a fire* – Industrious period ahead.

Police - *To see* – Alarming changes.
- *Justified arrest* – Unfortunate incidents.
- *Innocent arrest* – Overcome rivalry.

Polishing - *Any object* – Achieve enviable position.

Poor - *Yourself* – Insult but fortune will not be impaired.
- *Other* – Kindness.

Poppies - Desire to be free of responsibilities.

Pork - Sickness and misfortune.

Porter - Desire to travel.

Portfolio - Perplexities. Change of surroundings.

Postman - An important letter will come.

Post office - A task to be managed.

Pot - *To see* – Irritants to surface.
- *Boiling* – Pleasant duties to handle.
- *Broken* – Portends disappointments.

Potatoes - *Digging and finding* – Gain and Success.
- *Digging and not finding enough* – Ill-fortune.

Poultry - Selfishness detrimental to prosperity.

Powder - Do not be carried away by flattery.

Prayer - Health. Happiness but fear of failure.

Preacher - *To see* – Hurdled progress.
- *Yourself* – Losses and disharmony.
- *To hear* – Misfortune.
- *Walking away* – Affairs will move with new zeal.
- *Long haired* – Disputes with associates.

Preaching - Rise in position. Gain of strength.

Precipice - Forewarning to abandon present pursuits.

Pregnancy - Anxiety and impatience with conditions.

Pregnant woman - Good news.

Present - Loss in the future.

Priest - Desire to overcome wrong.

Primroses - Sickness, deceit, sorrow and grief.

Prince - Aspiration for better living.

Princess - Meeting with woman. Desire for good living.

Prison - *To see* – Change in course of life.
- *You are in* – Freedom. Happiness.
- *Putting someone in* – Invitation for wedding.

Procession - *To see* – Will be possessed by fears
- *Funeral* – Pleasure will be shadowed by sorrow.
- *To participate* – Foretells gaieties.

Profits - Success in immediate future.

Programme - You will realize your wishes.

Proposal - An engagement is indicated.

Prostitute - *In company of* – Defamation.
- *For young woman* – She will deceive her lover.
- *For married woman* – Quarrels.

Prostitution - Difficulties.

Provisions - *Abundance* – Competency.
- *Shortage* – Poverty and want.

Public house- *Keeping* – Will be compelled to act against your inclination.

- *Drinking at* – Sickness, poverty.

Pudding - *To see* – Small returns from large investment.
- *To eat* – Disappointments.
- *To prepare* – Lover not up to expectations.

Pulpit - *To see* – Sorrow.
- *To be in* – Sickness, failure in trades.

Pulse - *Yours* – Debilitating conditions.
- *Of others* – Committing depredations.

Puppet - Falsehood. Theft.

Puppy - Beware of gossip and petty quarrels.

Purse - *To see* – Financial loss. Desire for more property.
- *Find* – Happiness in love.
- *Lose* – Own sickness.

Pursuit - Determination to enjoy life.

Pyramid - *To see* – Change of venue for higher knowledge.
- *To scale* – Journey before reaching goal.
- *To study mystery* – Learning and honour.

Quack doctor - *To see* – Alarm over serious disease and its healing.

Quagmire - Difficulties and obstructions.

Quails - Bad intelligence and family shock.

Quarrelling - Should make new friends.

Quarrels - *To hear* – Complexities in leading life.
- *To participate* – Mismanagement at duty.

Quarry - Sudden and violent death of a close one.

Quay - Affairs will prosper.

Queen - *To see* – Happiness and prosperity.
- *You are* – Higher ambitions.
- *Frowns you* – Mother's affection.
- *Attending to* – Advancement to an honourable position.

Question - *To question* – Suspicion to overtake.

- *Being questioned* – Will face harrassment.
- *To ask* – Search for truth.

Queue - *To be in* – Disappointment.

Quicksand - *Be in* – Temptations and propensities to be evil.
- *Difficulty in coming out from* – Overwhelming ill-luck.
- *Being rescued* – Faithful lover.

Quilt - Sickness in the family.

Quinsy (tonsilitis) - *Being afflicted by* – Discouraging employment.
- *Others afflicted by* – The disease to cause anxiety.

Rabbit - *To see* – Desire to be strong.
- *For young people* – New friends of opposite sex.
- *For married people* – Will have children.
- *White* – Faithfulness in love.
- *Frolicking* – Children to contribute to your joys.

Race - Loss will be followed by a gift.

Radio - A letter informing an important event.

Raffle - Degraded habits. Loss of character. Ruin of business.

Raft - *Sail on* – Adventurous and successful journey.
- *Floating on* – Uncertain journeys.
- *To destination* – Good fortune.
- *Breaks* – Misfortune.
- *Sinks* – Loss and discredit.

Rage - Sincere and loving friends.

Rags - Beware of extravagance.

Rail road - *Winding tracks* – Intricacies in every phase of life.
- *Walking on* – Handle your affairs carefully.

Railway - A journey solving some of your problems.

Rain - *To see* – Your lover/life partner is affectionate and faithful.
- *Yourself in it* – Slowing up of plans.
- *Others in* – Will exclude friends from your trust.

- *Stormy* – Confusion of ideas.
- *Summer shower* – Foretells prosperity.
- *Escape being wet* – Your designs will mature soon.
- *To hear* – Domestic bliss and joy.
- *House leaking* – Illicit pleasure.
- *On farm stock* – Disappointments
- *To be soiled by* – Indiscreet indulgence.

Rainbow - *To see* – Hope and new beginnings.
- *For lovers* – Happy union.
- *Hanging low* – Success galore.

Raking - Success in undertakings and prosperity.

Rape - Desire for fulfilment of sexual love.

Rapids - Riding over or through rapids warns of negligence.

Raspberries - *Bush* – Many temptations.
- *Eating* – Gossip involving your reputation.

Rat - *To see* – Beware of your friends, there is an enemy among them.
- *To kill* – desire to be free from passionate alliance.

Ravens - Mischief is brewing. Trouble is coming.

Razor - *To see* – Good time is coming.
- *To cut yourself* – Unlucky for forthcoming deal.
- *Damaged* – unavoidable distress.

Reapers - Prosperity.

Red - Lucky colour for lovers. Vitality. Force of life. Festivity.

Refrigerator - *To see* – You will cause injury to right cause.
- *To put ice in* – Disfavours.

Religion - Violation of law.

Rent - *To rent a house* – Profitable agreement.
- *To fail to rent* – Inactivity.
- *To pay rent* – Financial interest will be safe.
- *Fail to pay* – unlucky.

Reprieve - Threre will be no pardon.

Reptiles - *To see* – Arguments. Deceit.
- *To kill* – Conflicting obstacles.
- *Bitten by* – Will suffer injury.

Rescue - *Others* – Rise in fortune.
- *Being rescued* – Suffer a slight loss.

Resign - *Yourself* – Unlucky efforts.
- *Others* – Unpleasant tidings.

Restaurant - Desire for socializing.

Revenge - Do not bear ill-will to others.

Revolver - *To hear* – Mismanagement.
- *To shoot* – Dishonour, sexual impulse.

Rhubarb - Opponents will favour.

Ribbons - Beware of treacherous deed.

Rice - *To see* – Steadfast friends. Wedding in family.
- *To eat* – Happiness.
- *To cook* – Future wealth.
- *To throw on bride and groom* – Desire to mate.

Rich - Will be poor for a long time.

Ride - *Yourself* – Unlucky for your business. Sickness.
- *Others* – Unpleasant tidings.

Riding - You will achieve your ambitions.

Riding school - *To visit* – Rising confidence.
- *To attend* – False friends.

Ring - *To see* – Generally lucky sign.
- *Wearing yourself* – Success in new business.
- *Wearing others* – Prosperity.
- *Hurts* – Illness of life partner.
- *Breaks* – Death of life partner.
- *Broken* – Separation from loved one.
- *To receive* – New devoted friend.
- *To give* – Newly found interests.
- *Selling* – Unhappiness.

Ringing	- Auspicious omen.
River	- *Clean* – Happiness. - *Calm* – Empty promises. - *Muddy* – Difficulties. - *Bathing in* – Recovery from disease. - *Drinking its water* – Promotion. - *Crossing it* – Will overcome difficulties. - *Waves on* – Troubles. - *Swim in* – Gain and respect. - *Fall in* – Worries. - *Drawn in* – Escape from criminal case.
Road	- *To see* – Strive to achieve your desired goals. - *Lined with trees* – Delightful surprise. - *Rough* – New enterprises. - *Drive on* – Indecision.
Robbed	- Losses.
Rock in chair	- *Be in* – Joy and contentment. - *Other person in* – Unexpected bliss. - *Empty* – Termination of an agreement.
Rocks	- *Climbing* – Disappointment. - *Descending* – Prosperity.
Rocket	- *Ascending* – Sudden and unexpected elevation. - *Falling* – Unhappy unions.
Roof	- *To be on top* – Chance to achieve success. - *To be reaching* – Struggle to reach goal. - *Building it* – Income augmentation through hard work.
Rook (bird of crow family)	- *To see* – Ultimate ambitions. - *A dead rook* – Sickness or death in near future.
Rooster	- *To see* – Happiness in home. Advancement. - *To hear* – Conceit. - *Fight* – Rivalry and altercations.
Rope	- *To see* – Happiness in the home.

- *Hang on to* – Concern about risky venture.
- *To climb it* – Perplexing complications.
- *To descend it* – Frustration.
- *To tie ropes* – Desire to rule others.
- *You are tied with* – Be careful in your dealings.
- *To jump over* – Physical need for change.

Roses
- *To see* – Love and admiration.
- *Together* – News of marriage.
- *White* – Illness in the family.
- *Red* – Festivity.
- *Yellow* – Spirituality.

Rowing - An important invitation that may indirectly help you.

Rubbish - An unexpected gift. Poor handling of affairs.

Ruins - Business difficulties in the near future.

Running
- *To see* – Not to succumb to temptations.
- *Self* – Wish for advancement.
- *With others* – Joy and festivity.
- *Away* – Fear of loss of money. Hatred.
- *Away with fear* – Free from difficulties.
- *You fall* – Beware of misfortune.

Rust - Destruction of property.

Sad - Great joy.

Saddle - Worries will fade away with a pleasant news.

Sadhu - Relief from worries.

Safe - Financial gain in business.

Sailing
- *To see* – Need to be alert.
- *In ship on smooth waters* – Prosperity.
- *In ship in rough waters* – Misfortune.
- *In small boat and reach harbour* – Rapid fortune.

Sailor - Changes in life. Voyage.

Sale - Monitor your financial transactions, not to be extravagant.

Salt - *To see* – Quarrels, dissatisfaction.
- *To eat* – desertion by lover.
- *To salt* – Harassment due to debts and mortgages.

Sand - *To see* – Your beloved is not quite reliable.
- *Walking on* – Quarrels.

Satan - Troubles.

Saw - *To see* – Will oversee a big project.
- *To use* – Happiness.
- *To hear* – Prosperity.
- *Rusty* – Failures.
- *Broken* – Accidents.
- *To carry* – Responsiblities and profits.
- *To find* – Restore your fortune.
- *To lose* – Disaster.

Scaffold - Imprudent actions will cause separation.

Scales - *Balancing* – Good judgement. Prosperity.
- *Girl weighs* – Faithful partner.

Scent - Respect. Happiness.

School - *To see* – Good luck associated with past event.
- *Attending* – Tensions need to be examined.
- *Revisit* – Frustration.

School teacher - *To see* – Interest in higher education.
- *Yourself* – Success in literary realm.

Scissors - *To see* – Jealousy and distrust of life partner.
- *For man* – Will have business success.
- *For girl* – May get engaged/married.
- *To lose* – Avoid disagreeable undertakings.

Scorpion - Gain of respect.

Scratch - *Yourself* – Need to clear debt.
- *Someone* – Misfortune.

Scream - *Yourself* – Accept the offer.
- *Hear* – Beware of friends.

Screw - A tedious task to be performed.

Sculptor - *To see* – Shift to less lucrative but distinguished position.
- *Yourself* – Change of occupation or decision.
- *Your lover* – Favours foretold.

Sea - *Voyage*. Success in your understandings.

Seal - Discontent.

Searching - Fear of a possible loss.

Seat - Making new friends.

Sea waves - Difficulties.

Selling - May lose a friend either temporarily or permanently.

Serpent - Argument and deceit. Conflicting obstacles.

Servant - *To see* – Beware of rumours. Association with wealthy.
- *Employ one* – Good fortune.

Seven - The number seven is lucky in dream.

Sewing - Difficulties are ahead, but you will overcome them.

Shadow - Quarrels. Loss.

Shake hands - Gain of object.

Shampoo - *Getting yourself* – Desire for secret rendezvous.
- *Others getting* – Not to repeat gossip.
- *To see shampooing* – Will be engaged in undignified affairs.

Shark - *To see* – Enemy.
- *Attacked by* – Despondency. Financial losses.

Shaving - Important business transaction. Long life.

Shawl - *To see* – Not to accept favours.
- *To lose* – Sadness.

Shears - Be careful in your dealings.

Sheaves - Favourable harvest. Prosperity and happy marriage.

Sheep - You will have an admirer. Good business and new plans.

Shell - Expect news from across the sea. Practise thrift.

Shelter - *Making one* – Plan to escape from enemies.
- *Looking for one* – May be deceitful.

Shelves - *Filled* – Good chance for material gains.
- *Empty* – Loss.

Shepherd - Success in trade.

Sheriff - Desire to be protected.

Ship - Will meet your love. Unexpected honour. Long journey.

Shipwreck - *Yourself in* – Misfortune.
- *Others in* – Elevation of friends or relatives.

Shirt - Temptation to commit adultery.

Shit - *To see* – Gain of wealth.
- *Touching* – Heavy gain of money.
- *To eat* – Find treasure.
- *To go for* – Wealth.

Shoe-maker - *To see* – Unfavourable for progress.
- *Yourself* – Employment opportunity.
- *Your lover is* – Wish fulfilment.

Shoes - *To see* – Busy days are ahead.
- *Getting shined* – Important changes are ahead.
- *Worn and dirty* – Be tolerant and thoughtful.
- *Untied* – Misfortune and quarrels.
- *Getting new pair* – Many journeys.
- *Soiled* – Enemies will emerge.
- *Blackened* – Eventful days ahead.
- *To lose* – Desertion and divorces.
- *Have been stolen* – Losses and gains.

Shooting - *To see* – Happiness.
- *A bird* – Success in business.
- *Miss* – Failure in business.

Shop - *Respect* – Conjugal partner.

Shopping - Success in business.

Shot - *You are shot* – fortells losses and despondency.

Shot gun - Dishonour.

Shovel - Hard work is required to achieve your goals.

Shower - *Of bath* – New pleasure.
- *Of rain* – Success in understanding of trade.
- *Of gifts* – Desire for change.

Sickness - Great temptation. Good health.

Silk - *Wearing clothes of* – Re-establishment of friendship.
- *Old* – Wealthy and elderly fiance.
- *Soiled and torn* – Presages disgrace.

Silver - *Small coins* – Distress.
- *Large Coins* – Lucrative business.
- *False* – False friend or lover.
- *In exchange for goods* – Prosperous trade.

Sin - *Commit* – Threat of troubles.
- *Resist* – Success. Happiness.

Singing - Warning for sorrows.

Skates - *Watch ice skaters* – Malicious gossip to damage reputation.
- *Watch youngsters* – Desire to share happiness.

Skeleton - *To see* – Enemies may inflict mental and financial troubles.
- *Haunts you* – Accident or death.

Skull - *To see* – Gain through will.
- *Leering* – Arguments and quarrels.

Sky - *To see* – Gain from son. Worldly pleasures.
- *Clear* – Desire to be with great people.
- *Fly towards* – Journey.
- *Reach* – Gain of object.
- *Float high in* – Disillusionment in love.
- *Clouds on* – Promotion and respect.
- *Red* – Social upheavels.

- *Fall from* – Disrespect. Demotion.

Slap - Victory over enemies. Gain of money.

Slaughter house - Sickness and heavy misfortune.

Slave - Worries. Journeys.

Sled - Imprudence in love affairs.

Sleep - Happiness.

Sliding
- *Yourself* – Success in business and affairs.
- *You fall* – Losses.
- *Someone trips you* – Beware of an enemy.

Slippers - Warning of intrigue and scandal.

Small pox
- *To see others with* – Sickness.
- *To see yourself* – Failure.

Smoke - Confused state of mind, quarrels.

Snail
- *To see* – Unhealthy environs.
- *To step on* – Will come across disagreements.

Snake
- *To see* – Sexual urge, worrries and grief, enemies.
- *To catch* – Victory over enemy.
- *To kill* – Escape from troubles.
- *To step on* – Grief or death.
- *In lap* – Worries from children.
- *In house* – Grief and worries from wife.
- *In hand* – Gain.
- *Bitten by* – Troubles and trauma.
- *Falling from roof* – Abuse from seniors.
- *Eat its meat* – Gain of wealth.
- *Shedding its skin* – Regeneration.
- *Two interwined* – Destruction and healing.
- *Cobra* – Success.
- *Black* – State honour and fame.
- *Golden* – Spiritual determination.

Sneezing - Success in efforts.

Snoring - Bright future.

Snow - *To see* – Lucky dream for young lovers.
- *Falling* – Disease. Emotional crisis. Loss of money.

Soap - Business difficulties. Beware of flattery. Restart.

Sold - *Anything* – Business worries.

Soldier - *To see* – Will be receiving news.
- *Marching* – Desire for advancement.
- *Wounded* – Bad judgement.
- *Yourself* – Will abandon your present job.

Son - *Obedient* – Craving for honour.
- *Unworthy* – Troubles.
- *Sick* – Losses.
- *Crying* – Difficulties.
- *Missing* – Anguish.
- *Rescued* – Danger will pass away unexpectedly.

Soot - Failures.

Soup - *To see* – Comforts.
- *To drink* – Temporary setbacks.
- *Others taking* – Good probability to marry.
- *To make* – Wealthy bridegroom.

Sovereign - *Yourself (ruler)* – Disgrace.
- *Find sovereigns (gold currency)* – Success.

Spade - Work hard for achieving prosperity.

Sparrows - Good fortune.

Spectacles - Rise in job or profession. Change of plan.

Speech - *To deliver* – Disputes.

Spider - *To see* – Success in all aspects of life.
- *Too many* – Responsibilities will overburden.

Spider web - Pleasant events.

Spit - Enhanced difficulties.

Splendour - Severe affliction.

Spools - With thread – Intricate tasks ahead.

	- *Empty* – Unsatisfactory results.
Spoons	- *To see* – Happiness at home.
	- *To lose* – Will be victim of suspicion.
Sport	- *Winning* – Misfortune.
	- *Losing* – Gain in near future.
	- *Watching* – Desire for harmony.
Spring	- *To see* – Success and long life.
	- *In house* – Happiness.
	- *In mountain* – Respect.
	- *Water* – Success. Happiness. Respect.
	- *Metal* – Hard decisions to be taken.
Spy	- *To see* – Anxiety.
	- *Yourself* – Misadventure.
Squirrels	- Rapid progress.
Stage	- Desire to be honoured and get prominence.
Stains	- *On yourself* – Worries over trifling difficulties.
	- *On others* – Betrayal.
Stairs	- *Falling down* – Be prepared for a disappointment.
	- *Walking down* – Bad luck in business and love.
	- *Ascending* – Good sign. Desire for sexual act.
Stamps	- You will make new friends.
Stars	- *To see* – Fulfilment of desires.
	- *Bright* – Prosperous years ahead.
	- *Dusky* – Mischief and deceit.
	- *Shooting* – Distress and despondency.
	- *Catching* – Happiness from son.
	- *Disappear* – Poverty and vexation.
Starving	- Success and plenty.
Stealing	- Desire to posses unattainable.
Steps	- *Walking up* – Urge for sexual intercourse.
	- *Walk down* – Bad luck in love and in business.
	- *To fall down* – Enemies will cause hurdles.

Stick - Work hard and happiness will be yours.

Sting - Being stung means injury by wicked person.

Stocking - Keep a check on frivolity.

Stones - Hindrances. Fear of some person.

Store - Pleasure in near future.

Storm - Quarrels ahead. Confusion of ideas. Gain.

Stove - Desire for warmth and protection.

Stranger - Many opponents.

Straw - Misfortune. Bad trade and lack of money.

Straw berries - Good luck in general.

Street - *Walking down* – Achieve something worthwhile.

Street poster - Disagreeable news.

Struggling - With burglar means honours.

Study - Happiness.

Stumble - *Fall* – Misfortune.
- *No fall* – Fortune in some undertaking.

Sugar - Ill health in the family. Irritable disposition.

Suffocated - Health and robustness.

Suicide - *To see* – Annoyance due to another person.
- *To commit* – Desire to escape burden.

Sun - *To see* – Meeting with a spiritual man: sage, saint.
- *Rising* – Good news. Happy times.
- *Setting* – Protect all your assets.
- *Overcast* – Troubles change.
- *Peeking through clouds* – Return of prosperity.

Swamp - *To see* – Uncertainly. Unhappiness.
- *To escape* – Problems will be solved.

Swan - *White* – Prosperity.
- *Black* – Not to get involved in vice or woman.

Sweeping - *Yourself* – Favours from family members.
- *Servants* – Contradictions.
- *Reluctance in* – Bad days ahead.

Sweet - *To eat* – Name and fame.

Sweetheart - *Beautiful and attractive* – Purity.
- *Pale and sick* – Falsehood.

Sweetener - Self-control.

Swimming - *Alone* – Success.
- *With others* – New friends.
- *Struggle in* – Difficulties.
- *Submerged in* – Unpleasantness.
- *In river* – Difficulties removed.
- *To watch* – Long life.

Sword - *To see* – Desire for sexual union. Win over enemy.
- *Carrying it* – Honour and fame.
- *Others holding it* – Defeat and failure.
- *Attack with* – Reunion in the family.
- *Snatched from you* – Anihilation.
- *Broken* – Despair. Disgrace.
- *Lose* – Loss of position.

Symphony - Occupation of liking.

Syringe - *To see* – False alarm regarding a relative's health.
- *Broken* – Disease and worries.

Table - *Setting* – Prosperity.
- *With food* – Urge for flattery.
- *Clearing* – Pleasure will turn to trouble.
- *Empty* – Poverty.
- *Eat at uncovered* – Independent disposition.
- *Eat at badly covered* – Altercations.
- *Broken* – Fortune to dwindle.
- *Stand on* – Indiscretions.
- *Rapping of* – Disorientation.
- *Moving* – Dissatisfaction.

Tacks - Annoyance.

Tailor - Will be having new clothes.

Tale - Ill-luck to come.

Talking - *Loudly* – Will have troubles.
- *About you* – Fortune will gladden you.

Tap - Running tap is unlucky.

Tar - Will soon be travelling.

Taxi - An important visit will soon be made.

Tea - *To have* – Good time.
- *Invitation for* – Accept it, will help you.
- *Making* – Indiscretions.
- *Drink* – Desire for change in environs, separation of loved ones.

Teach - Dream of teaching signifies a small loss.

Teacher - *To see* – Fortunate days ahead.
- *To talk* – Practical advice is required.
- *Yourself* – Desire to rule others.

Tears - Happy days are ahead.

Teasing - *You are* – Trouble and sickness.
- *Being teased* – Good news.

Teeth - *To see* – Desire for independence and nourishment.
- *Falling out* – Fear of old age and defamation.
- *White and beautiful* – Gratification of wishes.

Telegram - *To receive* – Disagreeable news.
- *To send* – Disappointments at home or in business.
- *Handling* – Fringe effects.
- *To see in post office* – Unfortunate engagement.

Telephone - *Talking on* – Increased resources.
- *Hear a ring* – expected call will follow.
- *To be aware of* – You need to be cunning.
- *To see* – Harassment from strangers.
- *Poor audibility* – Gossip and loss of friend.

Telescope - *Buy* – Change of heart.
- *Sell* – Strengthening of affection.

Television - Fame and recognition of talents.

Tempest - Much persecution but enemies can do no harm.

Temptation - Will win respect from known persons.

Tennis - *Playing* – Yearning for popularity.
- *Win* – Desire will be fulfilled.
- *Lose* – Hard work.

Tents - *New* – Loss, change of environment would be helpful.
- *Old* – Gain of wealth.

Terror - Someone trying for your downfall.

Tests - Experiencing some sort of ordeal and fear of failure.

Thatch - *House with straw* – Rise above present position.

Theatre - Hidden urge to be more important.

Thermometer - *Looking at* – Disagreements.
- *Rising mercury* – Will overcome failing fortunes.
- *Falling mercury* – Downfall in affairs.
- *Broken* – Sickness.

Thief - *To see* – Financial difficulties.
- *Yourself* – Strained social relations.
- *Pursue one* – Will overcome difficulties.
- *Capture one* – Overpower enemies.

Thimble - Insignificant anxieties.

Thorns - Difficulties ahead.

Thread - *To see* – Gain of money.
- *Tangled* – Overkindness.
- *Broken* – Losses.

Threshing - Success

Throw stones - Accusation.

Thunder - *With lightening* – Troubles ahead.
- *At distance* – will overcome all difficulties.

Tickle
- *Being tickled* – stream of worries.
- *Tickle others* – Loss of happiness through trivialities.

Ticks
- *To see ticks on your flash* – Poor health.
- *To mash a tick on yourself* – Irritation and treacherous foes.

Tiger
- *To see* – Cruelly and valour. Fear complex.
- *Approaching you* – Troubles and trauma.
- *Attacking you* – Failure and gloom.
- *Survive attack* – Good fortune.
- *You kill it* – Success.
- *Running away from* – overcome opposition and rise.
- *In caze* – Defeat your opponents.
- *Rugs of tiger skin* – Luxrious living.

Till
- *To see wealth in till* – Success.
- An empty till – Disappointment.

Timber
- Business and success.

Tipsy
- New friends will promote your welfare.

Toads
- *To see* – Ill disposed competition.
- *Kill* – Success and triumph.

To bacco
- *Others smoking* – Successful conclusion of tribulations.
- *Yourself smoking* – Desire for peace and harmony.

Toilet
- *To go for* – Litigation over money or properly.
- *Bowel movement* – Financial success.
- *Defecate* – Find treasure.
- *Faces* – Wealth and profit.
- *Excrement* – Elemination of emotions.
- *Urinate* – Release from tension and/or worry.

Tomato
- *To see* – Urge for socializing.
- *Ripe* – Happy married life.

Tombs
- *Walking among* – marriage.
- *Ordering your own* – Will marry shortly.
- *Fall into ruins* – Sickness and trouble.

Tongue
- *Long* – Victory over enemies.

	- *In pieces* – Disrespect.
Tools	- Hard work is ahead but it will be profitable.
Topaz	- *To lose* – Perjury.
	- *To obtain* – An interesting love affair.
Torpedo	- Desire to remove hurdles.
Torture	- A scene of torment in dream means bad luck.
Tower	- *To see* – Will aspire to high elevation.
	- *To ascend* – Reversal of fortune.
	- *Reaching top of* – Eventually fortune will smile.
	- *Fall from* – Disappointment.
Toy	- *To see* – Will soon hear of birth.
	- *Beautiful* – Happiness.
	- *Broken* – Sadness and complications.
Traffic	- *To watch* – Seek help for solving problems.
	- *To drive through* – Easement of family difficulties.
	- *Jam* – Patient efforts desired.
Train	- *To see* – Expect a journey.
	- *Sit in* – No travelling.
	- *Miss* – Disappointments.
Tram	- You will get the thing aspired.
Tramp	- A fear of failure.
Trap	- Difficulties unless you are careful.
Travel	- Evolution and change.
Travelling	- *Yourself* – Pleasure and profit.
	- *Through rough terrain* – High and lows of life.
	- *Through hills* – Advancement.
	- *Through woods* – Troubles and hindrances.
	- *In a car* – Eventful journey and worry.
Tray	- An important offer will be made to you soon.
Treasures	- Loss through confidence in somebody treacherous.
Tree	- *With leaves* – Will have many friends.
	- *Leafless* – Will make enemies.

- *With new foliage* – Satisfaction and success.
- *With leaves turning yellow* – Illness.
- *Straight* – Good news.
- *Wet* – Sex with a beautiful woman.
- *Thorny* – Disease.
- *Dead* – Loss and sorrow.
- *Sapling* – Poverty.
- *Climbing* – Success through your efforts.
- *Cutting* – Loss through mistakes.
- *Falling from* – Loss of employment.
- *Fallen* – Misfortune.
- *With fruits* – Wealth and fortune.
- *Taking fruits from* – Inheritance coming from elderly person.
- *Apple* – Fame.
- *Mango* – Birth of a child.
- *Christmas* – Happiness and joy.
- *Sleeping under* – Abandonment.

Trinkets - A good marriage.

Triplets - *To see* – Success in affairs where failure was feared.
- *Your wife has* – Happy end to entangled dispute.
- *To hear crying* – Resolving and reconciliation.

Troubles - Removal of worries.

Trout - Catching a trout means money.

Trumpet - *Blow* – Prosperity. Discomfiture of your foes.
- *Hear* – Troubles.

Trunk - A change of place is signified.

Tub - Filled with water – Fear of an evil.
- *Empty* – Troubles and misfortune.

Tumble - Loss of position and goods.

Tunnel - May have troubles or dificulties and will fade soon.

Turkey - Merry time is approaching.

Turnip - Riches. High employment. For lover fidelity.

Turtle - Business expension.
Tweezers - Abuses from friends.
Twine - Complications at working place.
Twins - Work hard and happiness will be yours.
Typing - Success in your business or profession.
Ugly - *Yourself* – Disputes with kith and kin.
- *Others* – Reproachment.

Ulcer - Unsatisfactory condition.
Umbrella - *To see* – Financial difficulties.
- *In rain* – A friend will help out.
- *Borrowed* – Sorrow and pain.
- *Lose* – Severe loss.

Uncle - A visitor will bring you good news.
Underwear - Will have new things in the house.
Un-dressing - Accept the invitation received, helpful to you.
Unhappy - *Being* – Brings good luck.
Uniform - Will realize your ambitions.
University - Achieve an ambition and gain fame.
Unpacking - Will have a holiday or a trip.
Urinal - Disorder in home affairs.
Urinate - Comforts through son. Release of worries.
Urine - *To see* – Increase of creative power and/or strength.
Urn - *To see* – Ups and down.
- *Broken* – Unhappiness.

Usurper - *Yourself* – Troubles.
- *Others* – Struggle and victory.

Vacant room - Financial gains.
Vaccinated - *Yourself getting* – Sorrows.
- *Others getting* – Declined contentment.

Valentine - Marriage proposal or an adventure.
Valley - Sickness followed by good health.

Van - Exciting times ahead leading to success.

Vase - *Of flowers* – Unexpected pleasures.
- *Broken* – Sorrow.

Vault - Good news.

Vegetables - *To see* – Will bring you luck.
- *Eating* – Small successful ventures.
- *Cooking* – Confusion.
- *Withered* – Sadness over trifling speculation.

Vehicles - *Car* – Your body is behaving like a car.
- *Train* – You have no control.
- *Bus* – Indicates status of your relation with others.
- *Boats* – Emotions you are navigating.

Veil - *To see* – Success.
- *Wearing* – May suffer because of your own insincerity.
- *Bridal* – New opportunity.
- *Mourning* – Embarrassing monetary troubles.

Veneer - Losing speculation.

Ventrilo-quist - Desire for feeling great.

Vermin - Loss of some sort.

Vessel - Partings are ahead.

Vexed - Will be gladdened by tidings of good fortune.

Vice - *Yourself indulging in* – Reputation in danger.
- *Others indulging in* – Misfortune for your friends.

Victim - *Yourself* – Victory of your opponents.
- *Other* – Wealth through wrong means.

Victory - Success, gain and vanquishing of enemies.

Villa - Will realise your wishes, perhaps change of abode.

Vineyard - *Good* – Favourable speculation.
- *Bad* – Disappointment.

Violence - *To feel* – Promotion to higher sphere.
- *To see* – Some unresolved anger.

- *Be victim of* – Conflicts in life.
- *In war zone* – You need to reconcile.
- *To commit* – desire for self-punishment.

Violets - Joyful occasions ahead.

Violin - *To see* – A good and gay time is ahead.
- *Playing* – Honours.
- *Broken* – Separation from a loved one.
- *Hear* – Will be guest of honour at a gathering.

Viper - Unfaithful partner and enemies to rise.

Vision - *To see a person* – The person to meet unexpected death.
- *To see places and property in* — Misery.

Visit - *To a friend* – Friend will recover from illness.

Visiting - An invitation to bring happiness.

Voice - *Many voices* – Listen to your innerself.
- *To hear pleasent* – Reconciliation.
- *To hear unpleasent* – Disappointment.
- *To hear weeping* – Anger will be stimulated.
- *To hear prophecy* – Spirituality will be heightened.
- *To hear own child* – Perplexity.

Volcano - Be careful of troubles and quarrels.

Vomitting - Death of near one.

Voting - Be careful of what you advise.

Voyage - *Good* – Inheritance.
- *Bad* – Incompetence.

Vulture - *To see* – Oppressing circumstances.
- *Wounded* – Limited damage.
- *Dead* – Escape from injury.

Wading - *Girl wading through smooth waters* – Will marry soon.
- *Girl wading through tempest* – Will form an illicit relation.

Wager - *Making one* – Indulgence in dishonest means.

- *Lose one* – Will sustain injury.
- *Win one* – Fortune.
- *Put up one* – Adverse circumstances.

Wages - *Have your wages* – More lucrative job.
- *Have been increased* – Will lose your job.

Wagon - Will have to take a journey.

Wail - Will have cause for joy.

Waiter - Gay times and plenty of invitations.

Waking up - Foretells happiness by return of loved one.

Walking - *Clean place* – Happiness and success.
- *In dirt* – Disappointments.
- *At night* – Fear of threatening circumstances.

Walls - *To see* – Will be head of a region. Hurdles.
- *Enclosed by* – Frustrations due to failures.
- *Breaking through* – Success in spite of obstacles.
- *Jumping over* – Tremendous effort for reaching goal.
- *Falling* – Loss of money.

Wallet - Financial security is sure.

Walnuts - Difficulties and troubles.

Waltzing (Dancing) - Happiness and pleasure.

Wandering - Your anxieties will soon pass away.

Want - *Yourself in* – Sorrow.
- *Contentment in* – Misery will fade away.
- *To relieve one* – Indifference.

War - Misfortune and unhappiness, family disputes, defeat.

Wardrobe - *Full* – Will receive a gift.
- *Empty* – Desire will not be realized.

Warehouse - Will have large possessions.

Warrant - Peace and respect.

Warrior - Change of employment.

Washing - Good times are ahead, will be busy by trifles.

Wasp - Increase in business.

Watch - *To see* – Good sign for those in love.
- *To check time* – Desire to do more in less time.
- *To break one* – Loss and trouble.
- *To lose one* – Domestic upheavals.
- *To steal one* – Cruel foe.
- *To present one* – Setbacks.

Water - *To see* – unexpected gain.
- *Flowing* – You are in for worries.
- *Calm and still* – There is sorrow ahead.
- *Rough* – Difficulties before success.
- *To play in* – Desire to be loved.
- *Running* – Gain of object.
- *Clear* – Philosophical or religious achievement.
- *Muddy* – Messy situation in real life.
- *Of rain* – Need to harmonise elements of your psyche.
- *Of sea* – Survival assured.
- *Of fountain* – Fortune.
- *Walk on* – Success.
- *Float on* – Happy news.
- *Drown in* – Worries. Do philanthropic work.
- *Drink* – Struggle for profession. Gain in work.
- *Drink hot* – Warning of disease.
- *Take out* – Gain of money.
- *Drawing from well* – You will be tormented by wife.
- *Collecting* – Good business.
- *Spraying* – Consummation of the awakened passions.
- *Pouring* – Loss of law suit.
- *Carry* – Difficulties.
- *Jump into* – Hope for another chance.
- *Flooding house* – Quarrels with an enemy.
- *Disappearance of* – Good times to come.

Water melon - *To eat* – Worries.

Waves - *Surrounded by sea waves* – Distressing circumstances.
- *Escape from* – Perseverance.

Waving - An invitation for visit.

Wealth - *To see* – Poverty.
- *To get* – Success. Rise in life.

Weapons - You have secret enemies.

Wear - *New clothes, shoes* – Happiness.
- *Old clothes, shoes* – Loss of money.

Weasel - *To see* – Beware of former foes.
- *To destroy* – Will survive schemes.

Weather - *To dream* – Undulating fortune.

Weaving - Success of your plans.

Web - Obstacles, worries.

Wedding - Happiness to come, luck for lovers.

Wedding-clothes - *To see* – New friends.
Soiled – Loss of a friend.

Wedding party - Worries, troubles.

Wedding ring - *To see* – Happy married life.
To lose – Sorrows.

Wedlock - *To dream of* – Disagreeable relations.

Weeding - Health, wealth and long life.

Weeping - To weep in dream brings happiness.

Weighing - *To dream of* – Success and prosperity.
- *Yourself* – Fulfilment of your wishes.
- *To weigh others* – Will win their loyalty.

Well - *To see* – Your friends are true to you.
- *Dig in house* – Wealth, promotion.
- *Fall in* – Worries.

Whale - A minor accident.

Wheat - Change in profession, retirement.

Wheel - *To see* – Prosperity is sure.
- *Rotating* – Agility and success.
- *Broken* – Loss of a family member.

Whip - Do not be hasty in words or deeds.

Whirlpool - *Being engulfed* – Adversity.

Whirlwind - Big trouble.

Whist (a card game) - *Playing whist* – Success in speculative activities.

Whistle - Will receive displeasing news.

White - Simplicity, spirituality, peace, purity.

Widow - *To see* – Poverty.
- *To become* – Child birth.

Wife - It is well said, "Happy will be the husband who dreams of his wife."

Will - Surprising events are likely to take place.

Wind - Disappointing events.

Wind Mill - *To see* – Changes in fortune for better.
- *Working* – Fortune.
- *Idle* – Adversity.
- *Broken* – Misfortune.

Window - Disappointing events.

Windstorm - Worries. Journey.

Wine - *Drinking alone* – Prosperity.
- *Drinking in company* – Your wedding feast.
- *Serving* – Lucrative business.

Wings - *On your body* – Rise in position and power.

Wire - Beware of quarrels.

Wireless - An event of importance likely to occur.

Wise Elder - *A magician* – Fantasies.
- *A priest* – Superiority.
- *A sage/saint* – Power.

Witchcraft - Misfortune.

Witness - Involvement in legal matters.

Wolf - Unprincipled friends and enemies.

Woman - *Young* – Happiness to children.
- *Old* – Happiness.

Woods - *Walking through* – Will be involved in mysterious events.
- *Green* – Will have lucky change.
- *Withered* – Calamity.
- *On fire* – Make plans for your welfare and security.

Wool - Be sure of peace and contentment.

Work house - Legacy will be bequeathed.

Working - *Hard* – Sickness.
- *With right hand* – Personal good fortune.
- *With left hand* – Momentary embarrassment.

Workshop - Will use all resources for betterment of an impending project.

Worm - Have disloyal friends, beware of them.

Wound - Happiness. Love.

Wounded - Prosperity.

Wreath - Will hear of or take part in wedding.

Wreck - Misfortune. Disappointment in love.

Writing - Yourself – Mistakes will be made.
Others – Embarrassing law suit.
Man – Rise in job.
- *Woman* – Will have proposal.
- *To read* – Will escape from enemies.

X-rays - Secrets will come to light.

Yacht - *To see* – Will make new friends, love of freedom.
- *Sailing* – Happiness.
- *Stranded* – Miscarriage of entertaining engagement.

Yardstick - Desire to be realistic and follow ideals of family.

Yarn - *To see* – A journey to prosperity.
- *For man* – Success in business.
- *For woman* – Suitable match.
- *Spinning* – Will receive a present.

Yawn - A journey is indicated.

Yawning - *Yourself* – Sickness, disease
- *Others* – Troubles for friends.

Yellow - *Bright* – Intuition. Faith. Health.
- *Dark/Muddy* – Secrecy. Betrayal. Avarice.
- *General* – Disappearance of troubles.

Yew Tree (a small tree with dark green leaves and red berries) - *To see* – Death of an elderly person leaving legacy for you.
- *Sit under* – Short life.
- *Gaze upon it* – Long life.

Young - *To see* – Domestic enjoyment.
- *Yourself* – Sickness. Dissolution.

Youth - *To dream of* – Lucky omen.

Zebra - Existing worries to fade away. Vivid ventures.

Zenith (highest point) - Prosperity.

Zodiac - *Twelve signs* – Travel round the world.

Zone (an area or a region) - Vexation. Loss of goods. Disappointment in love.

Zoo (Animals) - Do not be down-hearted, you will succeed when you expect least.

Zoological Garden - *To see* – Gain of knowledge; Sojourn in foreign countries.
- *To visit* – Ups and downs.

It is highly desireable to adopt the interpretation prudently and meaningfully; should that be not possible just forget it. If you have dreamed that something would happen, and it did, it is a coincidence, nothing more, despite all amazing stories to the contrary. How many times you have dreamed that something would happen and it didn't? If you are honest, you will admit that you remember your successes and conveniently forget your failures (which is of course desirable!).

The combinations of dreams and dream influences are as infinite as the stars, or the combinations of thought and number. They cannot be analysed in detail or as a whole. Dream "symbology" is a mystic foible forwarded to explain something which the mystics did not know anything about.

Every child is a born optimist; he has golden dreams. In youth he becomes still more optimistic. It is hard for a young man to believe that there is such a thing as death, such a thing as defeat or degradation. Old age comes, and life is a mass of ruins. Dreams have vanished into the air, and the man becomes a pessimist. Thus we go from one extreme to another, buffeted by nature, without knowing where we are going. Dreams may foreshadow the path.

Never mind, whether any of your dreams will ever be realized in this world; but sometimes it is better to dream a dream than die on hard facts. Great truths, even in a dream, are good, better than bad facts. So let us dream a dream.

Further, you are in the best position to interpret all the key words of your dream, synthesize the interpretation, and complete the dream work; thereby construct your dream vision or structure the whispers of your soul.

Epilogue

WE are concerned with the myriad games our psyche plays. We all know that there are regions of the human mind untrampled by the world of psychology, physics and technology. In the mystic sense of creation around us, in the expression of art, in a yearning towards God, the human mind-soul composite grows upwards and finds the fulfilment of something implanted in its nature.

Dreams clearly have a deep psychological core. This observation has been reported by psychoanalytic studies since the time of Freud. Accept your dream as a stimulating aperitif, and allow it to speak to you and reveal areas of your personality which you may not so far have appreciated. Learn, for instance, how to counter your weaker personality traits by using your more positive, strong qualities.

Dream symbols are produced spontaneously by ourselves, for ourselves, to convey special messages about the real state of affairs in the internal domain of our mind.

It seems very likely that current avenues of investigation of DNA and RNA will eventually show that certain types of dreams now classified as "clairvoyant," "precognitive," or "retrocognitive" are locked into one's genetic coding through the experiences or emotions of one's ancestors.

Dream analysis should basically be used to improve upon or to make progress or to have positive solutions to overcome difficult situations. Nonetheless, it is well established that dreaming is the best course for directing the "karmic" burden, much similar to the process of "Confession" or washing your sins by dipping into the river Ganges.

The day-dreams are productive if they are constructive, if they act as inspiration, and if they lead to action. Otherwise they are bad if they take the place of action. Too many of us learn to become satisfied by day-dreams; they become substitutes for the real things, and we find ourselves refusing to make the efforts or working towards reality.

By utilizing the information revealed by dreams imaginatively and consciously directing it into the future, a course of action can be plotted which leaves no room for failure. Unpredictable outcomes are transformed into inevitable successes, and life becomes a process of "Conscious enactment."

But see that you need not indulge in negative thinking and allow dark thoughts to cross your mind at all. In case of negativity getting dawned on your mind, take a deep breath in and hold it there as long as you can conveniently do so. You will find that all the thoughts have faded away. In case the thoughts are still persisting, repeat the "deep breathing and holding it" exercise a couple of times; the train of thoughts will be fully reoriented to fly high and hopeful.

Samuel Johnson wrote:

> The fountain of content must spring up in the mind, and he who has so little knowledge of human nature as to seek happiness by changing anything but his own disposition will waste his life in fruitless efforts and multiply the griefs which he purposes to remove.

As a human being, therefore, you can choose to either be part of the problem, or part of solution. Actually, unrealistic expectations fall into the category of crying for fuzzless peaches, stingless bees, or toasted snow. Perhaps they exist on other planets and in your dreams, but not on earth.

The main purpose of understanding dreams is to help one to formulate a strategy to free his/her FUTURE from "Fight or Flight" syndrome, and have a sense of the peace of mind.

The phenomenon of dreams is a baffling mystery. Sometimes they come true with stunning accuracy. But probability of such dreams is one in hundred thousands — the number of dreams one witnesses/ experiences during 60 to 70 years of his/her life. The occasional occurrence of the improbable does not imply the intervention of a higher power. . . . The term probability includes improbability at the extreme limits of probability, and when the improbable does occur this is no cause for surprise, bewilderment or mystification.

Still rare are the "enlightenment" dreams. They come as a bolt from the blue, only to one in ten million, and become the source of prophetic revelation. For example, Zoroaster (*c.* 628–551 BCE), a Persian, was a married man with children, before he received the revelatory message in the dream-trance from God, at the age of thirty. The angel Vohu Mana told Zoroaster that there is only one God, Ahura Mazda, and he must serve as His prophet. Zoroaster (Zarathustra) became the founder of an Iranian religion called Zoroastrianism.

The mystics do not dream, because they have no residuary thoughts that need to rise up in the form of a dream. J. Krishnamurti (1895–1986), a spiritual teacher, often remarked that he did not dream. Actually, he sort of "went over" the day mentally before going to bed every night — to "finish with it once for all" — a proces of "tying loose ends" to mop up any residuary thought before sleeping, and he believed that this was why he had no dreams.

Thus, the dreaming phenomenon can be controlled, as the dreams are the creation of human mind. The mind is the creation of God, which conceptualizes God. A God-gifted, organized, dreaming mind is triggered by unknown sensations during sleep; the sensations fire thoughts, the thoughts create ideations, imagination, intuition, and dreams. It suggests, God, mind, thoughts, and dreams are creative bright stars or black holes of cosmic consciousness.

Dreams have continued to wear their veil of mystery till very recently. Even now the veil has not been wholly lifted. However, dreams, consciousness, thoughts, emotions, feelings, body, mind, soul, and even God will continue to spin on the screens of science and spirituality forever.

The purpose of this book has been to highlight the scientific hue and spiritual avenue latent in dreams; the reader is requested to develop a forward-looking attitude and not be fadistic. Follow your conscious and conscience — ABRACADABRA.

Finally to conclude: "One can never attain immortality through the elixir tasted in a dream," said Jñāneśvar, boy-saint-poet, from India. Dreams are dramatic parapsychic events or displays of advaita (adualism/non-duality); where the actor, the action and the audience are one; seer-seen-seeing is one; and in this oneness is contained all.

Bibliography

Agarwal, Yatish, The World Within, Symptoms and Remedies of The Mind, New Delhi: Raj Kamal Books, 2004.

Ball, Pamela, Dream Dictionary, New Delhi: Academic Publishers, 2002.

Bedi, Ashok, Path to the Soul : The Union of Eastern and Western Wisdom to Heal Your Body, Mind and Soul, New Delhi: New Age Books, 2005.

Crookal, Robert, The Study and Practice of Astral Projection, London: The Aquarian Press, 1961.

Eeden, Frederic van, "A Study of Dreams", Proceedings of the Society for Physical Research; vol. 26 (1913).

Goldberg, Bruce, Soul Healing, New Delhi: Pustak Mahal, 1999.

———, Self-defence against Psychic Attacks and Evil Spirits, New Delhi: Pustak Mahal, 1999.

Hanger, Joan, Wake up to your Dreams, New Delhi: Penguin Books, India, 2001.

Heindel, Max, Occult Principles of Health and Healing, New Delhi: Cosmo, Indigo Books, 2002.

James, W., The Varieties of Religious Experiences, New York: New American Library of World Literature, 1958.

Joshi, Priya, Learn all about Dreams: the Virtual World, Delhi: Printline Books, and Tiny Tot Publications, 2004.

Kodikal, Deepa, A Journey Within the Self: A Diary of Yogic Experiences, New Delhi: Viva Book Private Ltd., 2006.

Koestler, Arthur, The Act of Creation, London: Pan Books Ltd., 1977.

Krishnamurti, J., The Flight of Eagle, Madras: Krishnamurti Foundation of India (KFI), 1982.

Kumar, Ravindra (Swami Atmananda), All You Wanted to Know about Dreams, New Delhi: New Dawn, and Sterling Publishers (P) Ltd, 2002.

Muldoon, Sylvan, and Hereward Carrington, The Phenomenon of Astral Projection, London: Rider and Company Ltd., 1951.

Nanda, Sunny, Dreams, The Truth Behind, Delhi: Raja Pocket Books, 2004.

Ouspensky, P.D., A New Model of the Universe, London: Routledge and Kegan Paul Ltd., (1960).

Raphael, Book of Dreams, Slough (U.K): W. Foulsham & Co. Ltd.

Reich, Peter, A Book of Dreams (Picador), London: Pan Books, 1975.

Robinson, Stearn and Tom Corbet, The Dreamer's Dictionary, The complete guide to interpreting your dreams, London: Chancellor Press, 2002.